The Hound of the Baskervilles

Sir Arthur Conan Doyle

Level 3
(1600-word)

Adapted by David Olivier

IBC パブリッシング

はじめに

　ラダーシリーズは、「はしご（ladder）」を使って一歩一歩上を目指すように、学習者の実力に合わせ、無理なくステップアップできるよう開発された英文リーダーのシリーズです。

　リーディング力をつけるためには、繰り返したくさん読むこと、いわゆる「多読」がもっとも効果的な学習法であると言われています。多読では、「1. 速く 2. 訳さず英語のまま 3. なるべく辞書を使わず」に読むことが大切です。スピードを計るなど、速く読むよう心がけましょう（たとえば TOEIC® テストの音声スピードはおよそ1分間に150語です）。そして1語ずつ訳すのではなく、英語を英語のまま理解するくせをつけるようにします。こうして読み続けるうちに語感がついてきて、だんだんと英語が理解できるようになるのです。まずは、ラダーシリーズの中からあなたのレベルに合った本を選び、少しずつ英文に慣れ親しんでください。たくさんの本を手にとるうちに、英文書がすらすら読めるようになってくるはずです。

《本シリーズの特徴》
- 中学校レベルから中級者レベルまで5段階に分かれています。自分に合ったレベルからスタートしてください。
- クラシックから現代文学、ノンフィクション、ビジネスと幅広いジャンルを扱っています。あなたの興味に合わせてタイトルを選べます。
- 巻末のワードリストで、いつでもどこでも単語の意味を確認できます。レベル1、2では、文中の全ての単語が、レベル3以上は中学校レベル外の単語が掲載されています。
- カバーにヘッドホーンマークのついているタイトルは、オーディオ・サポートがあります。ウェブから購入／ダウンロードし、リスニング教材としても併用できます。

《使用語彙について》

レベル1：中学校で学習する単語約1000語

レベル2：レベル1の単語＋使用頻度の高い単語約300語

レベル3：レベル1の単語＋使用頻度の高い単語約600語

レベル4：レベル1の単語＋使用頻度の高い単語約1000語

レベル5：語彙制限なし

CONTENTS

Chapter 1
Mr. Sherlock Holmes 4

Chapter 2
The Curse of the Baskervilles 7

Chapter 3
The Problem 14

Chapter 4
Sir Henry Baskerville 20

Chapter 5
Three Broken Threads 29

Chapter 6
Baskerville Hall 38

Chapter 7
The Stapletons of Merripit House 46

Chapter 8
First Report of Dr. Watson 56

Chapter 9
Second Report of Dr. Watson 60

Chapter 10
Parts of the Diary of Dr. Watson 71

Chapter 11
The Man on the Tor 78

Chapter 12
Death on the Moor 88

Chapter 13
Fixing the Nets 101

Chapter 14
The Hound of the Baskervilles 113

Chapter 15
Looking Back 122

Word List 128

読みはじめる前に

本作品は大きく3部に分けられます。各パートの内容を把握して、読者の皆さんも謎解きに参加してみましょう。

[1章〜5章] 舞台はロンドン。ホームズの事務所をモーティマー医師が訪ねてくる。聞けば友人のチャールズ・バスカヴィル卿の死に際し、その財産の受け取り人であるヘンリー・バスカヴィルをロンドンに迎えにきたのだが、バスカヴィル家にまつわる恐ろしい伝説のこともあり、そのままデボンシャーの屋敷に連れて行っていいものかどうか迷っているというのだ。この訪問からホームズとワトソンが事件に関わることになる。

[6章〜10章] ホームズの代わりにワトソンが、事件解明とヘンリー保護のためデボンシャーに赴くことになった。500年続く名家には、チャールズに仕えていた使用人のバリモア夫妻が住んでおり、ほかに近隣住人のステイプルトン兄妹、フランクランド親娘らが登場するが、誰もいわくがありそうに見える。正体不明の男の存在も浮かび上がってきた。ワトソンの推理はいかに進むのか。ホームズに報告するかたちで、ワトソンの推理が展開される。

[11章〜15章] ワトソンも予期せぬところから、ついにホームズが登場する。突然のホームズの出現に驚くワトソンだったが、ここから2人の謎解きが最終段階に入る。本当にバスカヴィル家の不幸は、魔犬伝説のせいなのか!? ヒューゴの悪事がめんめんとバスカヴィル家を呪い続けているのか。真相解明に乗り出すホームズとワトソンだったが、それには危険を伴う大きな賭けに出なければならなかった。

主な登場人物

Sherlock Holmes　シャーロック・ホームズ　冷静沈着で鋭い推理力を持つ探偵。

Watson　ワトソン　医師であり、ホームズのよき相棒。本作ではとくにワトソンの活躍が目立つ。

James Mortimer　ジェームズ・モーティマー　死亡したチャールズ・バスカヴィル卿の主治医であり、友人。

Charles Baskerville　チャールズ・バスカヴィル卿　デボンシャー州の富豪、バルカヴィル家の当主。ある日、死体で発見される。

Hugo Baskerville　ヒューゴ・バスカヴィル　チャールズの数代前のバスカヴィル家の統治者。残酷な荒くれ者。

Barrymore and his wife　バリモアとその妻　バスカヴィル家の使用人。先代からこの屋敷に勤めている。

Henry Baskerville　ヘンリー・バスカヴィル　チャールズ卿の弟（若くして死亡）の子供。唯一の遺産相続人。

Frankland　フランクランド　ラフターホール (Lafter Hall) の住人。趣味は望遠鏡で星をみること。嫁にいったローラ (Laura Lyons) という娘がいる。

Jack Stapleton　ジャック・ステイプルトン　博物学者、メリピット・ハウス (Merripit House) に美しい妹ベリル (Beryl) と住む。

Rodger Baskerville　ロジャー・バスカヴィル　チャールズ卿の一番下の弟。荒くれ者でヒューゴに似ていた。イギリスから南米に逃れ、家族もなく亡くなった。

Cartwright　カートライト　ホームズの手伝いをする少年。

James Desmond　ジェームズ・デスモンド　バスカヴィル家の遠縁にあたる聖職者。

Selden　セルデン　ノッティングヒル殺人事件の犯人。脱獄して逃走中。

Perkins パーキンス バスカヴィル家の御者。
Lestrade レストレード ホームズの長年の知り合いで警部。

単語・熟語リスト

本書で使われている用語です。わからない語は巻末のワードリストで確認しましょう。

p.7	curse	p.26	false
p.8	hound	p.31	suspect
p.8	evil	p.41	criminal
p.8	will	p.41	villain
p.8	cruel	p.47	deny
p.8	carry off	p.49	pity
p.9	moor	p.51	hut
p.11	baronet	p.54	duty
p.11	murder	p.70	convict
p.11	butler	p.89	uncover
p.12	heir	p.94	despair
p.13	property	p.95	evidence
p.16	well-being	p.97	deserve
p.22	clue	p.110	pass for
p.24	warn	p.126	carry out

Chapter 1
Mr. Sherlock Holmes

Mr. Sherlock Holmes was sitting at the breakfast table. I was holding the walking stick which a visitor had forgotten the night before. It was a good, thick piece of wood with a large, round head. There was a silver band around it on which was written, "To James Mortimer, M.R.C.S., from his friends of the C.C.H. 1884." Family doctors often carried such a stick.

"Well, Watson, we missed the visitor last night. We know his name but don't know why he came. Let's see what we can understand about him by studying his stick."

Holmes took the stick, walked to the window and studied it closely.

"I think he is a young doctor who worked at Charing Cross Hospital, but left the city to work in the country. I think he is friendly, not interested in

1. Mr. Sherlock Holmes

success, and forgetful. And he has a dog of average size."

I couldn't believe Holmes knew these things by looking at a stick. From my bookcase I took down the Medical Directory and found the name Mortimer. I read to Holmes.

"Mortimer, James, M.R.C.S., 1882, Grimpen, Dartmoor, Devon. House-doctor, from 1882 to 1884, at Charing Cross Hospital. Author of several papers about disease. Medical Officer for the counties of Grimpen, Thorsley, and High Barrow."

Holmes smiled knowingly. "In my experience only a friendly man receives gifts from co-workers; only a man not interested in success leaves a London practice for the country; and only a forgetful one who leaves his stick."

"And the dog?"

"The dog often carries the stick behind his master. Here are his teeth marks. They are about the size of a—yes, it is indeed a spaniel."

"My dear Holmes, how can you possibly know that?"

"Because I see the dog now on our door-step, and his master is ringing our bell. Let's find out what Dr. James Mortimer, a man of science, wants from Sherlock Holmes, the detective."

Our visitor didn't look like a country doctor. He was a young man, very tall and thin, with a long nose like a bird. He wore eyeglasses. His clothes were old. He walked with his head forward in a kind, curious manner. As he entered the room he noticed the stick in Holmes's hand, and ran towards it with joy. "Oh, I'm so very glad," said he. "I couldn't remember where I left it. I love that stick."

"Well, you are as we imagined you," said Holmes glancing at me. "And now, how can we help you?"

"I assume that you are Mr. Sherlock Holmes."

"That's correct. And this is my friend, Dr. Watson."

"I have heard of you both and am very glad to meet you. I am a humble man of science, Mr. Holmes. I have a particular interest in the brain."

Sherlock Holmes pulled up a chair for our strange visitor. "Did you come here last night and again today only to talk about brains?"

"No, sir, no. I came to you because I am faced with a very serious problem and you are a great detective."

"Tell me about your problem, Dr. Mortimer."

Chapter 2
The Curse of the Baskervilles

"I have a manuscript in my pocket," said Dr. James Mortimer.

"Yes, I can see a corner of it. I'm very good at dating manuscripts. I'd say that one is from 1730," said Holmes.

"Well done, Mr. Holmes. The exact date is 1742." Dr. Mortimer took it from his coat pocket. "Sir Charles Baskerville gave me this family manuscript. His death three months ago in Devonshire was very sudden and sad. I was his personal friend as well as his doctor."

Holmes reached for the manuscript and opened it. At the top was written: "Baskerville Hall, 1742."

"It appears to be a story."

"Yes, it is a tale about the Baskerville family. But it will help you to understand why I came here. I'd like to read it to you."

Holmes leaned back in his chair and listened. Dr. Mortimer began to read the following, strange tale:

"My sons, I come in a direct line from Hugo Baskerville. My father told me about the Hound of the Baskervilles, as his father had told him. I write this story now believing what I was told. I want you to believe that the evils of the past can be forgiven and changed. Learn from this tale so that the past tragedy of our family will not come again in our future.

"Many years ago this Manor of Baskerville was owned by Hugo. He was a wild and godless man, like others in the region, and he was also a very cruel man. Hugo fell in love with the daughter of a farmer who lived in the area. But the good, kind, young lady was afraid of him. One holiday the girl's father and brothers were away from home. Hugo knew this, so he went with a few of his bad companions to the farm and carried off the girl. They brought her to the Hall and locked her in an upstairs room. They then went downstairs to get drunk as they did every night. The poor girl upstairs was afraid but brave. She climbed out the window and escaped. Then she ran towards home across the moor.

"A short time later Hugo discovered she

2. The Curse of the Baskervilles

was gone. He was crazy with anger. He ran downstairs, jumped upon the table and shouted that he would give his soul to the devil in return for catching the girl. His drunken friends were surprised. One of them said they should let the hounds chase the girl. Hugo then ran outside and let the hounds go. He got on his horse and followed them across the moor in the moonlight.

"A while later his drunken friends got on their horses and rode toward the farmer's house. On the moor they passed one of the night watchmen. They asked him if he had seen the hunt. The man was so afraid that he could hardly speak. He said that he had seen the unhappy girl, the hounds chasing her and Hugo Baskerville on his black horse. 'But I have seen more than that,' said he. 'Running silently behind the horse was a huge hound. It must have been from hell because God could not have created such an animal.' At first the drunken men didn't believe him. But later they saw the frightened black horse without a rider. Soon they also saw the hounds standing together on a hilltop, making crying sounds.

"Now the riders were afraid. Finally they rode down the valley until they came to a broad open space. They saw two large stones, placed there hundreds of years ago by ancient people. The moon was shining brightly. The poor farm girl lay near the stones. She had died of fear. Near her lay the body of Hugo Baskerville. Standing over Hugo and tearing at his throat was a terrible black beast. It looked like a hound, but was larger than any dog alive. As they watched, the beast ate the neck of Hugo Baskerville. Then, with fiery eyes, it turned towards the men. They rode screaming across the moor. Their lives were never again the same.

"This is the tale, my sons, of the hound which has cursed our family ever since. I tell you this because I believe that it is better to know the truth than to hide from it. It is true that many in our family have died sudden, bloody, mysterious deaths. However, we must be good people and trust God to remove this curse from our family. Finally, my sons, please don't cross the moor at night when the powers of evil are greatest."

Dr. Mortimer finished reading this story and looked at Holmes.

"Very interesting," said Holmes.

Dr. Mortimer then took a newspaper article from his pocket.

2. The Curse of the Baskervilles

"Now, Mr. Holmes, here is something more recent. This is the *Devon Newspaper* of May 14th of this year. It is a short account of the facts of Sir Charles Baskerville's death."

Our visitor began to read:

"The recent sudden death of Sir Charles Baskerville is a tragedy for the county. The baronet was a very likeable and generous person who had many friends. He made his money in South Africa. Two years ago he brought that money to Devonshire when he moved into the family home. He had many ideas to improve Baskerville Hall and the county. Sir Charles had no children. He wanted to share his wealth with others.

"Sir Charles probably died of natural causes and was not murdered. There are old tales about the family history but they had nothing to do with his death. He was a man of simple tastes. He had only two housekeepers, Barrymore the butler and his wife. They said that Sir Charles was not very healthy. Dr. James Mortimer, his friend and doctor, also said he had a weak heart.

"The facts of the case are simple. Sir Charles Baskerville took a walk along the path of yew trees every night. On May fourth Sir Charles told Barrymore that he was going to London the next day. That night he went out for his usual evening walk, smoking his usual cigar. He never returned. At midnight Barrymore became worried and went to search for him. He could follow Sir Charles's footprints on the wet path. Halfway down the path there is a gate which leads out onto the moor. It appeared that Sir Charles had stood at the gate for some time. His body was discovered at the end of the path. Barrymore says that his master's footprints changed after he passed the moor gate. There were no marks of any kind on the dead man's body. However, there was a terrible look of fear on his face. Both Dr. Mortimer and the police doctor believe that he died of a heart attack. Now the foolish tales of evil can be ended and the next heir can move into Baskerville Hall. That person is Mr. Henry Baskerville, son of Sir Charles Baskerville's younger brother. The young man lives in America."

Dr. Mortimer said, "Those are the public facts of Sir Charles's death."

"I see," said Sherlock Holmes. "Now please give me the private facts."

2. The Curse of the Baskervilles

Dr. Mortimer seemed emotional. "There are few people who live on the moor. Everyone there knows each other. I often saw Sir Charles Baskerville. Only two other men who live there, Mr. Frankland of Lafter Hall, and Mr. Stapleton, the natural scientist, are well-educated. Sir Charles and I became friends because of his illness, and because we love science.

"In recent months Sir Charles's nervous condition became worse. He truly believed this tale and the terrible curse of his family. He was afraid to walk upon the moor at night and never left his own property. Often, he thought he heard strange creatures at night.

"I suggested that Sir Charles go to London because he needed a city holiday. And then came this terrible night.

"The night Sir Charles died Barrymore the butler sent for me. I got to Baskerville Hall less than an hour after he found the body. I checked all the facts, including the footsteps down the path. I was also the first one to examine the body. His face was so changed by fear that I hardly recognized him. There were no marks on his body. I also clearly saw something near the body that no one else saw—the footprints of a giant hound!"

Chapter 3
The Problem

I could see the excitement in Holmes's eyes at these words.

"You said nothing? Why did no one else see it?"

"The marks were about twenty yards from the body. I'm sure I noticed them only because I'd heard the tale. The prints were huge."

"But it did not come near the body?"

"No."

"What kind of night was it?"

"Wet and cold."

"What is the path like?"

"There are two lines of old yew trees. They grow like a wall and are about twelve feet high. The path in the center is a strip of grass on both sides between the trees and path. There is a gate which leads to the moor about halfway along the path."

3. The Problem

"Is there any other opening to the path?"

"None. Only from the house."

"Tell me, Dr. Mortimer, were the footprints you saw on the path or the grass?"

"The path. You can't see any prints on the grass."

"Were they on the same side of the path as the moor gate?"

"Yes, they were on the edge of the path on the gate side."

"Very interesting. Was the gate closed?"

"Closed and locked."

"How high was it?"

"About four feet high."

"Then anyone could climb over it?"

"Yes."

"And what marks did you see by the wooden gate?"

"It seems that Sir Charles had stood there for several minutes."

"How do you know that?"

"Because the ash from his cigar had dropped twice."

"Good detective work, Doctor. But I wish I had been there. I would know exactly what happened."

"However, Mr. Holmes, there are some things even you cannot know."

"Do you believe that this thing is supernatural?"

"I don't know anymore. Before Sir Charles died several people said they saw a huge, devilish creature on the moor. People are very afraid and nobody will cross the moor at night."

"You are a scientist. Do you think it comes from hell?"

"I honestly don't know."

Holmes sighed. "Dr. Mortimer, if you believe such supernatural stories then why did you come to me?"

"It's about the young heir, Sir Henry Baskerville."

"Is he the only heir?"

"Yes. Sir Charles had two younger brothers. The second brother died young. He was the father of Henry. The third, Rodger Baskerville, was the family bad boy. They tell me he looked and acted like old Hugo. He had to escape from England and ran to Central America. He died there in 1876 of disease. Henry is the last of the Baskervilles. I must meet him at Waterloo Station in one hour. Now, Mr. Holmes, what should I do?"

"I think he should go to his family home."

"Yes, he probably should. The well-being of the entire county depends upon the wealth of the

3. The Problem

family. But every Baskerville who goes there meets an evil fate. This young man is the last heir. I need your advice."

Holmes thought for some time.

"I suggest that you take a cab to Waterloo and meet Sir Henry."

"And then?"

"Say nothing to him until I make a decision about the matter."

"How long will that be?"

"Twenty-four hours. Please return here with Sir Henry at ten o'clock tomorrow."

"All right, Mr. Holmes." He began to leave.

"Only one more question, Dr. Mortimer. Did anyone see this creature on the moor after Sir Charles died?"

"I don't think so."

"Thank you. Good morning."

Holmes returned to his seat with a satisfied look on his face.

I knew that my friend needed to be alone. He wanted to smoke tobacco and think about the case. I spent the day at my club and returned to Baker Street at nine o'clock that evening. The room was completely filled with smoke.

"I see you have been inside all day," I said.

"My body remained in this armchair, but my

mind went to Devonshire. Here is a large map of the area, and here is Baskerville Hall in the middle."

"There are woods around it?"

"Yes. This is the small village of Grimpen, where Dr. Mortimer lives. As you see, there are only a few other buildings in the area. These are farmhouses. Here is Lafter Hall and there is a house which may be the home of Stapleton, the natural scientist. Then fourteen miles away is the great prison of Princetown. All around these points is the lifeless moor. It's the kind of place a devil would enjoy——"

"Then you too believe in this supernatural idea?"

"No. I believe that people can be devils. There are two questions to begin with. The first, whether or not there has been any crime; the second, what is the crime and how was it done? Have you thought about the case?"

"Yes, all day long. It's very strange, indeed. For example, why do you think his footprints changed down the path?"

"He was running, Watson—running for his life. He ran until his heart stopped and he fell dead."

"Running from what?"

"I don't know yet. But I think he was very afraid of something that came from the moor. I also think

3. The Problem

he was waiting for someone."

"Why do you think so?"

"The man was old and not healthy. The weather was bad. Why would he stand in one place for five or ten minutes?"

"But he went out every evening."

"Yes, but he usually avoided the moor and probably the gate. That night he waited there. It was the night before he went to London. This case interests me, Watson."

Chapter 4
Sir Henry Baskerville

Our guests arrived at almost exactly ten o'clock. The young heir was a small man with dark, intelligent eyes, about thirty years old. He had a strong-looking body and face. He appeared to be both a man of the outdoors, and an English gentleman.

"This is Sir Henry Baskerville," said Dr. Mortimer.

"Yes," he said, "and I'm glad to meet you, Mr. Holmes. I understand that you enjoy puzzles. I've already had one this morning."

"What happened?"

"Nothing very important, Mr. Holmes. It was this letter I received this morning."

He put the letter on the table. The address, "Sir Henry Baskerville, Northumberland Hotel," was printed with a rough hand. It was post-marked, "Charing Cross," with yesterday's date.

4. Sir Henry Baskerville

"Who knew that you were going to the Northumberland Hotel?" asked Holmes, looking at our visitor.

"Nobody. Dr. Mortimer and I decided to stay there only after we met."

"Hmmm! Someone seems to be interested in where you go." He unfolded the letter. In the middle of the paper was a single sentence made up of printed words placed together. It said:

If you value your life or your reason keep away from the moor.

Only the word "moor" was written by hand.

"What does this mean, Mr. Holmes?" asked Sir Henry Baskerville.

"Well, Dr. Mortimer, there seems to be nothing supernatural about it."

"What are you talking about?" asked Sir Henry sharply.

"I promise you, Sir Henry, that you will know as much as we do before you leave this room," said Sherlock Holmes. "For now, let's think only about this very interesting note. It must have been put together and posted yesterday evening. Do you have yesterday's *Times* newspaper, Watson?"

"Yes, here it is."

His eyes quickly ran up and down the pages. "I see that the words in this letter and the print in the newspaper are the same. Someone cut out those words from yesterday's paper."

"You're right! That's very clever!" cried Sir Henry.

"Well, this is my special interest. I have studied the differences in newspaper type for years. The *Times* is like no other print."

"But why was the word 'moor' written by hand?" asked Sir Henry.

"Because the other words were all simple to find in a newspaper. But 'moor' is less common, and this person could not find it in print."

"What else do you see in this message?"

"There are one or two other clues. The address, for example, is written in rough characters. I think the writer is trying to hide his own handwriting because you may recognize it. Also, the *Times* is a paper usually read by educated people. So I assume that the letter was created by an educated man. Further, you see that the words are not arranged in a straight line. I believe he was in a hurry when he did this because he wanted it to reach Sir Henry quickly."

"Surely, Mr. Holmes, you are only guessing now," said Dr. Mortimer.

4. Sir Henry Baskerville

"I don't like the word guess. Rather, I begin with real facts and use science in my thinking. And one more thing; I feel certain that this address was written in a hotel."

"How on earth can you say that?"

"Look closely and you will see that the writer had difficulty with the pen. A private pen is usually full and working well. But as you know, in hotels it is uncommon to find a good pen. Yes, I really think that we should look in the hotel waste-baskets around Charing Cross until we found the same copy of the *Times*. Then we could easily find our writer. Whoa! What's this?"

He was examining the letter paper, holding it close to his nose.

"Well, what is it?"

"Oh, nothing," he said suddenly, putting it down. "I think there is nothing more to learn from this strange letter. So, Sir Henry, what else has happened to you since you came to London?"

"Well, there is one small matter. I've lost one of my shoes."

"Please tell me about it," said Holmes.

"Well, yesterday I went shopping because I needed new clothes. Among other things I bought some expensive brown shoes. They needed a special oil to make them soft so I put them outside my door last night. This morning there was only one. The man who cleans them didn't know anything about it. The worst part is that I never had a chance to wear them."

"Interesting," said Sherlock Holmes. "Perhaps you'll find the missing shoe when you return to the hotel."

"I hope so. Now, gentlemen," said Sir Henry, "please keep your promise and tell me what's going on here."

"All right," Holmes answered. "Dr. Mortimer, I think you ought to explain the story to Sir Henry as you did to us."

Then our friend of science took his papers from his pocket and repeated what he had told us. Sir Henry Baskerville listened closely until he finished.

"Well, I'm in an interesting situation. Of course, I've heard of the hound since I was a young boy. It's a favorite family story. But I never thought it was serious. My uncle's death is a real mystery, isn't it?"

"Yes."

"And now someone sent this letter to me at the hotel."

"Perhaps, someone is kind enough to warn you of danger," said Holmes. "Or they may be trying to frighten you for their own purposes. But now we

4. Sir Henry Baskerville

must decide, Sir Henry, whether or not you should go to Baskerville Hall."

"I've already decided. There is no devil in hell, Mr. Holmes, and there is no man on earth who can stop me from going to my home. And that is my final answer." He had the forceful voice and strong temper of the Baskervilles. "Right now," said he, "I would like to have an hour or two to think about all that has happened. Mr. Holmes, why don't you and Dr. Watson come have lunch with us at two o'clock. We can talk further then."

"Fine, you may expect us at two. Shall I call a cab for you?"

"I'd prefer to walk in the fresh air. Good day."

Our visitors left the house. Instantly, Holmes said, "Quick, get your hat and coat, Watson! We must follow them!" We hurried down the stairs and into the street. Dr. Mortimer and Baskerville were about two hundred yards ahead of us.

"It is a very fine morning for a walk, Watson. I want to follow our friends but I don't want them to see us."

We continued into Oxford Street and down Regent Street. That's when Holmes noticed the cab across the street with a man inside. When our friends stopped, the cab stopped. When they moved, it moved.

"He's our man, Watson! Come on! We'll have a good look at him."

At that instant I saw a face with a large black beard inside the cab. He looked at us through the window. He then shouted to the driver, and the cab drove quickly down Regent Street. Holmes looked quickly for another cab but saw none. He then chased the cab down the street, but was already too far behind.

Holmes was upset. "Bad luck and bad planning, too. It was my fault! I should have stayed behind the cab. Now we have lost him."

"Who was the man?"

"I have no idea. But I knew that someone was following Baskerville. That's how this person knew they were at the Northumberland Hotel. This man is very clever, Watson, and I don't know yet whether he wants to hurt or to help us."

"Too bad we didn't get the cab number!"

"My dear Watson, it was number 2704."

We were standing on Regent Street. Dr. Mortimer and Sir Henry were no longer in sight.

"There's no point in following them now," said Holmes. "The mystery man is gone. Did you see his face inside the cab?"

"Only that he had a large beard."

"Yes, it was probably a false beard to hide his

4. Sir Henry Baskerville

face. Come in here, Watson!"

Holmes walked into one of the local messenger offices. He was greeted by the manager.

"Ah, Mr. Holmes, how can I help you?"

"Does that boy named Cartwright still work for you?"

"Yes, sir, I'll get him."

"Thank you! And I would like to change this five-pound note."

A boy of fourteen, with a bright face, was called in by the manager. He stood looking with great respect at the famous detective.

"Let me have the Hotel guide book," said Holmes. "Thank you! Now, Cartwright, there are the names of twenty-three hotels here, all in the area of Charing Cross. Do you see?"

"Yes, sir."

"Here is what I want you to do. You will visit each hotel. You will give the doorman one shilling. Here are twenty-three shillings."

"Yes, sir."

"Tell him that you want to see yesterday's wastepaper. Tell him that an important telegram was lost and that you are looking for it. But you are really looking for a page of the *Times* with some holes cut in it. Here is a copy of the *Times*. Can you recognize it?"

"Yes, sir."

"It will be a difficult job and you probably won't find it. But try your best. Here are ten extra shillings in case you have any problems. Send me a report at Baker Street before the evening. And next, Watson, we will send a wire to find out who was cab driver number 2704."

Chapter 5
Three Broken Threads

At two o'clock we arrived at the Northumberland Hotel.

"Sir Henry Baskerville is expecting you," said the front desk man.

We walked up the stairs. Sir Henry was standing there, his face was red with anger. He was holding an old, dirty shoe.

"What's the matter?" asked Holmes.

"These hotel people must think I'm a fool," he cried. "This is a bad joke. If that man can't find my missing shoe there will be trouble."

"Are you still looking for your shoe?"

"Yes, sir, but this time it's an old black one."

"What! You don't mean —— ?"

"That's just what I mean. I only had three pairs of shoes in the world—the new brown ones, the old black ones, and the special leather ones which I'm wearing now. Last night they took one of my brown ones, and today they took one of the black. Well, have you got it? Speak, man!" said Sir Henry to a nervous German worker.

"No, sir. I have asked all over the hotel, but nobody knows about it."

"I'm going to tell the manager."

"Please be patient, sir. I promise we will find it."

"Excuse my anger, Mr. Holmes. This is one of the strangest things that has ever happened to me. What do you think of it?"

"Well, Sir Henry, I'm not sure yet. I've handled many cases, but yours is one of the most difficult I've faced. Sooner or later we will know the truth."

The four of us talked during lunch.

"I'd like to go to Baskerville Hall at the end of the week."

"I think that's a good idea," said Holmes. "Did you know that someone was following you and Dr. Mortimer?"

Dr. Mortimer sat up surprised.

"Followed! By whom?"

"I don't know. Do you know anyone in Dartmoor who has a full, black beard?"

"No—or, um, let me see—why, yes. Barrymore, Sir Charles's butler, has a full, black beard."

5. Three Broken Threads

"Ha! Where is Barrymore?"

"He is in charge of the Hall."

"We should find out if he is really there, or if he is in London."

"How can you do that?"

"Give me a telegraph form." Holmes then wrote: 'Is all ready for Sir Henry?' "That will do. What's the nearest town? Grimpen? Good, we will send this to the postmaster in Grimpen and ask him to deliver it directly to Barrymore at Baskerville Hall. If he's not there then the postmaster will return the message here to Sir Henry."

"Very well," said Baskerville. "Dr. Mortimer, who is this Barrymore?"

"He is the son of the old housekeeper, who is dead. He and his wife are respected in the county."

"Did Sir Charles leave any money to Barrymore?" asked Holmes.

"He and his wife received five hundred pounds each."

"Ha! Did they know that they would receive this?"

"Yes, Sir Charles was very happy to talk about his will. Please don't think of everyone who received money from Sir Charles as a suspect. He also left a thousand pounds to me."

"Really! And anyone else?"

"There were many smaller amounts that went to different people. The rest went to Sir Henry."

"And how much was the rest?"

"Seven hundred and forty thousand pounds."

Holmes raised his eyes in surprise. "My, that's a large amount!"

"Sir Charles was richer than we knew. The total value of his possessions was nearly one million."

"Dear me! That's enough to make someone play a serious game. I must ask one more question, Dr. Mortimer. If anything happened to our young friend here who would become heir to the property?"

"Well, Sir Charles's younger brother, Rodger Baskerville, died unmarried. So the property would go to the Desmonds, who are distant cousins. James Desmond is an old churchman in Westmoreland. I have met him. He is an intelligent, honest man. I don't think he cares about money. But he would be the heir unless Sir Henry wants to change the will."

"And have you made your will, Sir Henry?"

"No, Mr. Holmes, I've had no time. But my uncle believed that the money should go with the title and the property. I feel the same."

"Well, Sir Henry, I agree with you about going to Devonshire without delay. However, you must not go alone."

"Dr. Mortimer will return with me."

5. Three Broken Threads

"But Dr. Mortimer is busy with his practice. And I am very busy here in London. You need a trusty man who will always be near you. My friend Watson is perfect for the job. Well, Watson, what do you think?"

I was very surprised. But before I had time to answer Baskerville was shaking my hand.

"Well, that is really kind of you, Dr. Watson," said he. "I will be very grateful to have your company at Baskerville Hall."

I have always enjoyed adventure. I also felt pleased by Holmes's words and the eagerness of Sir Henry.

"I will come, with pleasure," said I.

"And please report very carefully to me," said Holmes. "Then let's meet at the ten-thirty train from Paddington on Saturday."

As we stood up to leave Baskerville gave a little cry of joy. He reached under the bed and pick up a new brown shoe.

"My missing shoe!" he cried.

"That's very strange," Dr. Mortimer remarked. "I searched this room carefully before lunch."

"And so did I," said Baskerville. "There was no shoe then."

"Probably the worker found it and put it there while we were eating."

We sent for the German but he said he knew nothing about the shoe. No one else in the hotel knew either. Here was another mystery which had happened in the past two days. The others included the printed letter, the black-bearded man in the cab, the loss of the new brown shoe, the loss of the old black shoe, and now the return of the brown shoe. Holmes sat in silence in the cab. I knew he was thinking deeply about all these odd facts.

Just before dinner two telegrams were brought to us. The first said:

> Have just heard that Barrymore is at the Hall.
> BASKERVILLE.

The second:

> Visited twenty-three hotels as directed, but sorry to report no *Times* paper with cut-outs.
> CARTWRIGHT.

"There go two of my clues, Watson. We must look around for others."

"We still have the cab driver."

"Exactly. I have already sent for him."

At that moment, the doorbell rang. A rough-looking man entered. He was indeed the cab driver.

5. Three Broken Threads

"In the office they told me that a gentleman at this address was asking about No. 2704," said he. "Is something wrong?"

"There's nothing wrong, my good man," said Holmes. "In fact, I have half a pound for you if you will give me a clear answer to my questions."

"Well, what was it you wanted to ask, sir?" said the cab driver with a smile.

"First of all what's your name?"

"John Clayton."

"Now, Clayton, tell me all about the passenger who came and watched this house at ten o'clock this morning, then followed two gentlemen down Regent Street."

The man looked very surprised. "Well, sir, he told me he was a detective, and that I was to say nothing about him to anyone."

"Did he say anything more?"

"He mentioned his name."

Holmes glanced happily at me. "Oh? That was foolish. What was his name?"

"His name," said the cab driver, "was Mr. Sherlock Holmes."

Never have I seen my friend more surprised. For a moment he sat in shock. Then he began to laugh.

"Ah, Watson, he certainly fooled us this time,

didn't he? So, his name was Sherlock Holmes. Excellent! Tell me where you picked him up and all that happened."

"He got in my cab this morning. He offered me two pounds if I would do exactly what he wanted all day. I agreed. We went to the Northumberland Hotel. Two gentlemen came out and we followed them here. We waited an hour and a half. Then we followed them again along Regent Street until the man told me to drive quickly to Waterloo station. There he paid me, and told me, 'By the way, I'm Mr. Sherlock Holmes.' Then he walked into the station."

"And how would you describe Mr. Sherlock Holmes?" asked Holmes.

The cab driver seemed uncertain. "Well, I'd say he's about forty years old, of average height—shorter than you, sir. He was dressed like a rich man, and he had a black beard. His face was pale. That's all I can remember."

"Well, then, here is your half-pound. Thank you and good night!"

"Thank you, sir!"

John Clayton departed happily. Holmes turned to me with a slightly disappointed smile.

"There goes our third clue. We end where we began. Our bearded friend is very clever. He knew

5. Three Broken Threads

about us so he told the driver that he was me. I tell you, Watson, this case will not be easy. Please be very careful in Devonshire."

Chapter 6
Baskerville Hall

Sir Henry Baskerville and Dr. Mortimer were ready to take the train to Devonshire on Saturday. Mr. Sherlock Holmes drove with me to the station.

"I will not tell you my theories of the case, Watson," said he. "Rather, I want you to simply report the facts to me, as completely as possible."

"What kind of facts?" I asked.

"Anything which may affect the case. I am quite sure that Mr. James Desmond is not a part of this case. That leaves the people who live with or near Sir Henry Baskerville on the moor. We have a list of suspects. There are the Barrymores. There is our friend Dr. Mortimer, whom I believe is perfectly honest. There is this scientist, Stapleton, and his sister, a young lady. There is Mr. Frankland, of Lafter Hall, who is also unknown to us, and there are one or two other neighbors. These are the

6. Baskerville Hall

people whom you must study."

"I will do my best."

"Do you have your guns?"

"Yes."

"Good. This may be a dangerous case. Always be careful."

Our friends were waiting for us outside our first-class car.

"No, we have no news of any kind," said Dr. Mortimer when Holmes asked him. "I am sure that nobody followed us these past two days."

"Did you find your other shoe?"

"No, sir, it is gone forever."

"Indeed. That is very interesting. Well, good-bye." As the train began to move away he added, "Sir Henry, remember one of the sentences in that queer old tale which Dr. Mortimer read to us—avoid the moor in those hours of darkness when the powers of evil are strongest."

I looked back and watched the tall, straight, figure of Holmes standing at the station.

The journey was fast and pleasant. In a very few hours we were in the rich, green farmland of Devonshire. The cows were eating the tall grass in the fields. Young Baskerville was excited by the scenery.

"I've seen a lot of the world since I left here, Dr.

Watson," said he; "but I've never seen a prettier place."

"And I never met a Devonshire man who didn't love his county," said I.

"When was the last time you saw Baskerville Hall?" asked Dr. Mortimer.

"I've never been there. I was a teenager when my father died. We lived on the South Coast. From there I went straight to a friend in America. This is all new to me. I can't wait to see the moor."

"Well, wait no longer, for there is your first sight of the moor," said Dr. Mortimer, pointing out of the train window.

We looked out over the green squares of the fields and trees. In the distance was a gray, dark hill with a strange shape. It looked like scenery in a dream. Baskerville stared at it eagerly for a long time. It was his first sight of the land where his family had lived for centuries. He sat there in his American suit, with his American manners and way of speaking. But I knew that he was truly of this land. He had the family in his blood. There was pride and strength in his green eyes, his Celtic nose, and firm mouth. The moor might be dangerous, but he would be brave.

The train arrived at a pretty country station. People helped us carry our bags to a waiting wagon.

6. Baskerville Hall

Our driver was an old, small man. Soon we were driving down the wide white road. We passed farms, animals, houses and gentle hills in the warm afternoon sun. But behind that quiet countryside were those dark, rocky, evil-looking hills in the distant moor.

The wagon turned into a narrow, curving road. Autumn leaves fell from the many trees. The sun was setting. There was a steep curve in the moor road. On the point above us stood a horse and rider watching. He was a serious-looking soldier with a rifle.

Dr. Mortimer asked the driver, "Who is he?"

"There's a criminal who escaped from Princetown Prison a few days ago. He's a really dangerous villain. The guards watch every road. No one has seen him yet."

"Who is he, then?"

"He's Selden, the Notting Hill murderer."

I remembered the case well because Holmes was interested in it. The killer was a truly hateful, evil person with no respect for life. Our wagon came to the top of the rise and we could see the moor clearly. A cool wind began to blow. Somewhere out there was an evil murderer hiding like a wild beast.

The farmland was now behind us. The scenery

in front of us grew wilder and darker. There were huge rocks on the hillside. Occasionally we passed a house built of stone. Suddenly we saw two high, narrow towers above the trees.

"Baskerville Hall," said the driver, pointing.

Sir Henry stood up and stared with shining eyes. A few minutes later we passed through the iron gate into the tree-lined avenue. Baskerville looked up the road to the house at the far end.

"Was it here?" he asked in a low voice.

"No, no, the yew path is on the other side."

The young heir glanced around with a sad face. "It's dark here. I'll soon brighten this place with electric lights."

We came to Baskerville Hall. The center of the house was a heavy, old building with ancient twin towers. To the right and left of the towers were more modern wings of black stone. A soft light was shining through the windows.

"Welcome, Sir Henry! Welcome to Baskerville Hall!"

A tall man stepped from the entrance to open the wagon door. A woman also came out to help with our bags.

"Sir Henry, my wife is expecting me at home," said Dr. Mortimer. "I'll say good-bye and leave you with Barrymore."

6. Baskerville Hall

The wagon drove back out to the road while Sir Henry and I turned into the hall. The heavy door closed behind us. It was a fine building, we were in with large, high rooms of black oak. A warm fire was burning in the great old fireplace. It felt good because we were cold from the long drive. On the oak walls were family signs and animal heads.

"It's just as I imagined it," said Sir Henry with a big smile. "My family has lived in this same house for five hundred years. It makes me very proud."

Barrymore returned from taking our bags to the rooms. He stood in front of us now with the manner of a well-trained butler. He was a very good-looking man, tall with a square black beard and pale, strong features.

"Would you like dinner at once, sir?"

"Is it ready?"

"In a very few minutes, sir. You will find hot water in your rooms. My wife and I will be happy, Sir Henry, to stay with you until you have found new housekeepers. I'm sure that you will be needing more people to work."

"What do you mean?"

"Well, sir, Sir Charles led a quiet life. My wife and I were enough to care for the house. I'm sure you will want to have more company and will need more housekeepers."

"Do you mean that you and your wife wish to leave?"

"Only when it is convenient to you, sir."

"But your family has been with us for many, many years. I would feel badly if you left."

I could see the emotion on the butler's white face.

"My wife and I also feel that way, sir. But we were both very attached to Sir Charles. His death shocked us and made this house very painful to us. I'm afraid we shall never again feel comfortable in Baskerville Hall."

"But what do you intend to do?"

"I'm sure we shall succeed in one business or another. Sir Charles was very generous and we have enough money to live. And now, sir, may I show you to your rooms?"

Two sets of stairs went up to the second floor. There, two long hallways continued the whole length of the building. All the bedrooms opened on to these hallways. My room was near Sir Henry's in the same wing. This part of the house was newer and brighter.

But the dining room was a shadowy, unhappy room. It was too big for just two people. We were both silent. Old portraits of family members stared down at us from the walls. I was glad when the meal

6. Baskerville Hall

ended and we moved to the smoking room.

"Well, it isn't a very cheerful place," said Sir Henry. "Perhaps I will get used to it. I understand why my uncle was nervous living here alone. I think we should go to sleep early tonight and start fresh in the morning."

I tried to sleep but turned in my bed awake for a long time. I heard the wind blowing outside. Then suddenly, in the dead of night, I heard the clear sound of a woman crying. She couldn't control her sorrow. She was certainly inside the house. When it stopped I waited for half an hour, my nerves wide awake. But there was no other sound except the wind.

Chapter 7
The Stapletons of Merripit House

The following morning was fresh, beautiful and sunny. We felt much better about Baskerville Hall.

"I guess we were just tired and cold from the drive last night!" said Sir Henry as we ate breakfast together.

"Probably," I answered. "Tell me, did you hear a woman crying in the night?"

"Actually, I thought I heard something when I was half asleep."

"I clearly heard a woman crying."

"We must ask about this right away." He rang the bell and asked Barrymore if he knew anything about the crying. The housekeeper's face seemed to turn more pale as he listened to the question.

"There are only two women in the house, Sir Henry," he answered. "One is the kitchen-maid, who sleeps in the other wing. The other is my wife,

7. The Stapletons of Merripit House

and I can tell you that it was certainly not her."

But he was lying. For after breakfast I met Mrs. Barrymore in the bright hallway. She was a large woman with heavy features. Her eyes were red and larger than normal. It was she who cried long and hard in the night. Her husband must have known, yet he denied it. Why? There was already an air of mystery around this pale, handsome, bearded man. He was the one who discovered the body of Sir Charles. Was it Barrymore we saw in the cab? The cab driver had described a shorter man, but he might have been mistaken. I decided to go see the Grimpen postmaster, and find out if Barrymore had received the test telegram.

Sir Henry was busy with papers and work after breakfast. I took a pleasant walk of four miles along the moor's edge to a very small village. The postmaster was also the village storekeeper. He remembered the telegram.

"Certainly, sir," said he. "This is my son James. He delivered it to Mr. Barrymore."

"Into his own hands?" I asked the boy.

"Well, he was upstairs at the time, so that I could not put it into his own hands. But I gave it to Mrs. Barrymore, and she promised to deliver it."

"Did you see Mr. Barrymore?"

"No, sir. I told you he was upstairs."

"If you didn't see him, how do you know he was upstairs?"

"Well, surely his own wife should know where he is," said the postmaster, somewhat upset. "Didn't he get the telegram? If there is any mistake it is for Mr. Barrymore himself to tell me."

I decided not to ask any more questions. Clearly, we could not be certain that Barrymore was at home and not in London. I walked back thinking about the case.

Suddenly I heard the sound of running feet behind me and heard a voice call my name. I turned around. I didn't know him. He was a small, thin, clean-faced man with golden hair, between thirty and forty years of age. He was dressed in a gray suit and country hat. He carried a net for catching insects and a box to put them in.

"Please excuse me, Dr. Watson," he said. "I am Stapleton, of Merripit House. I was visiting Mortimer when you walked by his house. I wanted to introduce myself."

"How do you do," said I.

"I trust that Sir Henry is feeling fine after his journey?"

"He is very well, thank you."

"We were all afraid that Sir Henry might not want to live here after the tragedy of his uncle. Of

7. The Stapletons of Merripit House

course you know the tale of the devil dog which attacks the family?"

"I have heard it."

"Surprisingly, many country people here believe the story. Some say they have seen the creature on the moor. I think Sir Charles believed the tale and died because of it. Maybe he really saw something that night in the yew path. What do you think?"

"I honestly don't know."

"What about Mr. Sherlock Holmes?"

I was greatly surprised to hear my friend's name.

"Dr. Watson, everyone around here knows about your great detective friend. Your name is also well known. If you are here then it follows that Mr. Holmes is interested in the matter. I am curious to know what he thinks."

"I can't answer that question because he's busy in London with other cases."

"What a pity! I would like to talk to him. Please tell me if I can be of any help to you in this case."

We came to a narrow, grassy path that crossed the road into the moor. There was a sharp hill with many large rocks to the right. In the distance was a house.

"That is Merripit House," said he, "where I live with my sister. Would you like to meet her?"

I knew that Holmes wanted me to meet the neighbors so I agreed.

"It's a wonderful place, the moor," said he, looking around the hills and rocks and plants. "It contains so many secrets."

"You know it well, then?"

"I've only been here two years. We came shortly after Sir Charles moved in. Because of my interest in nature I have walked around almost every part of this country. I'm sure that few men know the area better than I do."

"Is it hard to know?"

"Very hard. That is the great Grimpen Mire. A mire is a place of wet, soft, bottomless ground," said he. "A wrong step there means death to man or beast. Today I saw a young moor horse die in there. It is always dangerous to cross it. But I have found one or two paths across the mire."

"Why do you want to go there?"

"Because the most uncommon plants and insects are in those hills."

"Perhaps I shall try one day."

"Dear God, don't even think of it," said he. "You would be lucky to come back alive."

"Whoa!" I cried. "What is that?"

A long, low, animal-like cry swept over the moor. It became a roar filling the air, then slowly ended.

7. The Stapletons of Merripit House

"The country people say it is the Hound of the Baskervilles calling for its food."

I looked around, a great fear in my heart.

"Surely you don't believe those tales. What do you think made such a sound?"

"I really don't know," said Stapleton. "The moor is a strange place."

As we continued walking on the path I saw a hill covered with unusual stone circles.

"What are those?"

"They are the stone huts of ancient men who lived here thousands of years ago. There are walls but no roofs."

"What did those ancient people do?"

"They raised sheep and cows on these hills. They learned to dig for metal. Look at the great hole they dug on the other hill."

Just then a small insect flew by, and Stapleton chased after it with great speed. I watched him running, jumping and hopping across the mire. Then I heard the sound of footsteps behind me. I turned and saw a woman near me. She had come from the Merripit House path.

I was sure that this was Miss Stapleton. She was a very beautiful woman, and very different from her brother. He was of light color, fair hair, and gray eyes. She was tall, with dark eyes and very dark hair. And her dress was also beautiful. She walked quickly towards me.

"Go back!" she said. "Go straight back to London, immediately."

I stared at her in stupid surprise. She was very serious.

"Why?" I asked.

"I cannot explain," she quickly whispered. "Please God, I'm warning you. Leave and never come back here."

At that moment Stapleton returned from chasing the insect and his sister became quiet.

"Hello Beryl!" said he. His voice was not very friendly.

"Hello Jack," she answered. "I was just saying hello to Sir Henry."

"No, no," said I. "I'm only his friend. My name is Dr. Watson."

A puzzled look came over her face. "Well, excuse my error," she said.

Her brother looked at us with questioning eyes.

"Perhaps Dr. Watson would like to see our house," she then suggested. A short walk brought us to it. It was an old farm house recently rebuilt. The outside of the house seemed lonely and cold but the inside was much nicer. The butler greeted us. He was a strange, very old man in a reddish coat.

7. The Stapletons of Merripit House

I looked out the window at the boring moor. I could not understand why this well-educated man, and this beautiful lady wanted to live there.

"It's a strange place for a house," said Stapleton as if reading my mind. "And yet we're quite happy here, aren't we Beryl?"

"Quite happy," she said, but her words sounded empty.

Stapleton said, "I had a school in the north. I loved teaching young people. However, we had some bad luck. There was a serious disease that occurred in the school and three of the boys died. The school closed and I lost a great deal of money. I miss teaching but I feel very lucky to live in this natural place."

"Isn't life a little dull for you here?" I asked Miss Stapleton.

"No, no, we are never bored," her brother answered.

"We have our studies, our books, and we have interesting neighbors like Dr. Mortimer. Poor Sir Charles was also an excellent companion. We were hoping to meet Sir Henry today."

"I'm sure he would be delighted."

"Meanwhile, please come upstairs and look at my excellent insect collection. Then we shall have lunch."

But I was eager to return to my duties. The sadness of the moor, the strange roar we heard earlier, and the serious warning from Miss Stapleton all made me uneasy. I excused myself and said good-bye.

To my surprise I saw Miss Stapleton waiting for me along the path. She had taken a shorter route to meet me.

"I must tell you quickly, Dr. Watson, that I'm sorry for my mistake," said she. "Please forget what I said."

"But I can't forget, Miss Stapleton," said I. "I'm Sir Henry's friend. What danger is there to him? Please be honest with me."

For a moment I could see in her eyes that she wanted to tell me something important. But then she said, "Oh, it's nothing; just a feeling I have. We were very shocked by Sir Charles's death, Dr. Watson. When he died I thought the tales of the hound might be true. I was upset when Sir Henry came here because I don't want him to be hurt."

"I don't believe those tales. Tell me, Miss Stapleton, why are you worried that your brother will see you talking to me?"

"My brother is very anxious for someone to live in the Hall. He thinks it will be good for the poor people in this county. He would be very angry if he

7. The Stapletons of Merripit House

knew I wanted Sir Henry to leave. Now I must say good-bye." She turned and walked quickly toward the house. With my soul still full of uneasy fears I returned to Baskerville Hall.

Chapter 8
First Report of Dr. Watson

Baskerville Hall, October 13th.

MY DEAR HOLMES:

Here on the moor I feel as if I have left modern England behind. It's a place with many ancient huts, graves and temples. I think there are many strange mysteries here.

I am writing this report to tell you what I have observed until now.

There is a dangerous criminal on the moor who escaped from prison two weeks ago. It seems impossible that this villain could live on the moor alone all this time. Most people believe he is no longer in the area.

Our friend, Sir Henry, is showing great interest in his lovely neighbor, Beryl Stapleton. She is very different from her brother. On the outside Stapleton

8. First Report of Dr. Watson

seems very cool and without emotion, but I think there is a fire burning inside him. He has much control over his sister.

He came over to visit Baskerville that first afternoon. The next morning he took us to see where the story of the evil Hugo took place. The scene was just as we heard it described in the story. There was a grassy area in a small, rocky valley with two old, tall stones that looked like the teeth of a beast. Sir Henry was very interested in all of it.

On our way back we stopped for lunch at Merripit House. That is when Sir Henry met Miss Stapleton for the first time. Both of them appeared to like one another. Since then we have seen the sister or the brother almost every day. Stapleton should be happy about a match between his sister and Sir Henry. However, I feel certain that he doesn't want them to fall in love. By the way, it will be very difficult for me to always stay with Sir Henry if a love affair develops.

On Thursday Dr. Mortimer and the Stapletons lunched with us. Sir Henry asked the doctor to take us to the yew path and show us exactly what happened that night. We all still have many questions about Sir Charles's death.

I have met one other neighbor since I last wrote; Mr. Frankland, of Lafter Hall. He is an older man, red-faced, white-haired. His passion is for the British law, and he spends most of his time and money in court. He's a queer old character who makes us laugh. His hobby is studying the stars with a telescope. Lately, he likes to use his powerful telescope to search for the escaped criminal on the moor.

Now, let me end by telling you about the most important development.

It concerns Barrymore. We can't be certain that he was here when you sent the test telegram. However, Sir Henry and I spoke to him and we believe that he was at the Hall and not in London. Sir Henry was kind to him and even gave him a gift of clothing.

Mrs. Barrymore is of interest to me. She is a heavy, hard-working woman who seems unemotional. Yet I have seen tears on her face several times. Something troubles her deeply.

You know that I am a light sleeper. Last night, at about two in the morning, I heard someone walking in the hallway near my door. I quietly looked out and saw a man holding a candle. He was walking softly, without shoes. From behind he looked like Barrymore.

I followed him. He entered one of the rooms at the end of the hallway. These rooms are completely empty. I quietly looked into the room.

8. First Report of Dr. Watson

Barrymore was standing near the window with the candle held against the glass. He seemed to be staring out onto the moor, waiting for something. Several minutes passed then he put out the light. I returned quickly to my room. This morning I talked to Sir Henry about it. We have a plan to discover this mystery. I will tell you about it in my next report.

Chapter 9
Second Report of Dr. Watson

THE LIGHT UPON THE MOOR

Baskerville Hall, October 15th.

MY DEAR HOLMES:

I know I didn't send you much news in the first days of my visit. But now things are happening quickly and there is much to tell.

The following morning I went to the room where I had seen Barrymore that night. The window in that room has the best view of the moor in the house. Therefore, I believe that Barrymore was looking for something, or someone out on the moor. The night was very dark, however, so I doubt that he could see anyone.

I told the baronet about it. He was less surprised than I expected.

"I knew that Barrymore walked around at night,"

9. Second Report of Dr. Watson

said he. "Two or three times I have heard his steps in the hallway at that hour."

"Perhaps he goes to that room every night," I suggested.

"If so, we should follow him and see what he's doing."

"But surely he would hear us."

"The man does not hear well. Besides, we must take a chance. We'll sit up in my room tonight and wait until he passes." Sir Henry rubbed his hands with pleasure. I could see he enjoyed the adventure.

These days the baronet is talking with designers and builders from London. He plans to spend a lot of money to restore the glory to Baskerville Hall. Then he will only need a wife to make it perfect. It's clear that he is very interested in Miss Stapleton. And yet, the road to love is not always smooth.

Today, for example, Sir Henry prepared to go out and I did the same.

"What, are *you* coming, Watson?" he asked, looking at me strangely.

"Well, you know that Holmes was serious when he told me to stay with you on the moor."

Sir Henry put his hand on my shoulder and smiled. "My dear fellow," he said, "I'm going to see Miss Stapleton and I prefer to go alone. I hope you understand." Before I could answer he opened the door and was gone.

I was in a difficult position. I decided it was best to follow him at a distance.

I hurried along the road toward Merripit House and turned onto the moor path. I climbed a small hill and saw him about a quarter mile away. He was talking to Miss Stapleton. I felt badly about spying on him, but I also had to protect him.

I watched Sir Henry put his arm around Miss Stapleton. Then it looked like he wanted to kiss her but she put up her hand to stop him. Then I noticed someone else walking towards them on the same path. It was Stapleton with his insect net. They both quickly turned around when they heard Stapleton approaching. He was angry. I guess that Sir Henry tried to explain the situation. The lady stood by silently. Finally Stapleton turned quickly and ordered his sister to follow him. She obeyed her brother and walked away. Stapleton appeared to be angry with her too. The baronet watched them leave, then walked back down the path, his head hanging sadly.

I ran down the hill and met the baronet at the bottom. His face was red.

"Hello, Watson! Where did you come from?" he asked.

9. Second Report of Dr. Watson

I explained everything to him. How I felt wrong about letting him go to the moor alone, how I followed him, and how I had seen everything. For a moment his eyes burned with anger, but my honesty softened him and he laughed a bit.

"I never thought it would be so difficult to carry on a private love affair here on the moor. I think her brother is crazy. How about you?"

"Not really."

"No, he probably isn't. But now I don't understand anything. What's wrong with me, anyway? Do you think I would make a good husband to the woman I love?"

"Certainly."

"Then why is he against me? It can't be my title or my house. I would never hurt his sister. He won't even let me hold her hand."

"Did he say so?"

"That, and more. Watson, I know she's the right woman for me. We make each other happy. But he will never let us alone together. This was the first time we tried. She was glad to see me but she didn't want to talk about love. She kept telling me that this was a place of danger and that I should escape. I said I might agree to leave only if she came with me. That is when her brother arrived like a madman. He was white with anger. I told him that I had true and honorable feelings towards her, and wanted to marry her. That made him angrier. I too was angry. It ended badly as you saw. I just don't understand it, Watson."

Neither did I. Everything about our friend—his fortune, his title, his age, his character, his appearance—is positive. However, later that same afternoon Stapleton came to the house to tell the baronet that he was sorry for his actions. They had a long talk in Sir Henry's study and came out friends once more. We are invited to dinner at Merripit House next Friday.

"He may be a bit crazy," said Sir Henry, "but he was kind to come and say sorry."

"Did he explain why he got so angry?"

"He said his sister is everything in his life. They've always been together and he doesn't like the thought of losing her. He didn't know that we were falling in love and he was shocked when he saw us together. He now feels very badly for his actions. He thinks I am a good match for his sister, but he needs some time to get used to the idea. So he wants me to wait three months before I ask to marry her. I promised to agree."

So there is one of our mysteries cleared up. I've also learned the secret of the Barrymores, which I will now report to you.

9. Second Report of Dr. Watson

Sir Henry and I sat quietly in my room last night with the lights very low. The hours passed slowly. Shortly after two o'clock we heard someone walk by in the hallway. We waited a moment then opened the door and followed him very quietly to the same room as before. For several minutes we watched him hold a candle to the window, moving it slowly back and forth.

Sir Henry walked into the room. Barrymore jumped up in great surprise, his eyes full of fear.

"What are you doing here, Barrymore?"

"Nothing, sir." He was so nervous that he could hardly speak. The candle was shaking in his hand. "I was just closing the window, sir."

"Don't lie to us, Barrymore!" said Sir Henry without patience. "Why were you holding a candle to the window?"

"Please don't ask me, Sir Henry—don't ask me! I give you my word, sir, that it is not my secret, and I cannot tell it."

A sudden idea occurred to me and I took the candle from him.

"I think the candle is a signal to someone out there," said I. "Let's try it." I held the candle and slowly moved it as I stared into the dark night. And then I saw a tiny yellow light from far off.

"There it is!" I cried.

"No, no, sir, it is nothing!" the butler broke in. "Believe me, sir——"

"Now, Barrymore," demanded the baronet, "Speak up! Who is that person and what is going on?"

The man refused to talk. "It is not my business and I cannot tell."

"Then you no longer work for me as of now. You have broken our trust and must leave without honor."

"Very well, sir. If I must, I must."

"No, no, sir! Please, it's not his fault, it's mine!" It was the voice of Mrs. Barrymore standing at the door in her nightclothes. She looked pale and afraid. "Sir Henry, my husband only wanted to help me because I asked him."

"Speak out, then! What does it mean?"

"My unhappy brother is living on the moor without food. We cannot let him die at our very gates. This candle is a sign to him that food is ready, and his light tells us where to bring it."

"Then your brother is——"

"The escaped criminal, sir—Selden."

"That's the truth, sir," said Barrymore.

Sir Henry and I both looked at her in shock. Could this good woman really have the same blood as one of England's worst criminals?

9. Second Report of Dr. Watson

"Yes, sir, my name was Selden, and he is my younger brother. We were too nice to him when he was a boy and spoiled him badly. He grew up thinking everything was for him. Later he met some really evil companions. He became a criminal, broke my poor mother's heart, and ruined our good name. But to me, sir, he was always my curly-haired little brother. He escaped from prison because he knew I was here at Baskerville Hall and that I would help him. He came one night hungry, cold and wet, with the prison guards after him. What could I do? We brought him in and took care of him. Then you returned, sir, and my brother thought he would be safer out on the moor. So he has been hiding out there since. Every second night we take out bread and meat for him. I want him to go away, but as long as he is there I have to help him."

We believed the woman and felt sorry for her.

"Well," said Sir Henry, "I cannot blame you for defending your own wife. Forget what I have said. We shall talk again in the morning."

When they were gone we looked out of the window again. Sir Henry had opened it and the cold night wind blew on our faces. Far away in the blackness there burned the tiny candle.

"How far do you think it is?" asked Sir Henry.

"Not more than a mile, I think."

"That villain is waiting by the candle. By God, Watson, I'm going to get that man!"

I was thinking the same thing. The Barrymores had admitted their secret to us, though not because they wanted to. This man was a danger to society. It was our duty to help put him back in prison before he hurt someone else.

"I will come, too," said I.

"Then get your gun and your coat."

In five minutes we were outside the door. The falling leaves were blowing in the autumn wind. Occasionally we saw the moon through the clouds. The candle light in front still burned.

"Are you armed?" I asked.

"I only have this hunting whip."

"We must take him quickly and by surprise."

"Watson, do you remember what Holmes said about the hour of darkness when the power of evil is strongest? Could this be it?"

Suddenly, at that moment, we heard that strange, ungodly, animal cry which I had heard near Grimpen Mire. It was a long, deep sound followed by a great roar, which slowly disappeared. The baronet took my arm and his face was white.

The night became silent again.

"Dear God, Watson! That was the cry of a hound," said the baronet.

9. Second Report of Dr. Watson

My blood ran cold for there was fear in his voice.

"What do people here call this sound?" he asked.

"Oh, they are simple people. Does it really matter?"

"Tell me, Watson. What do they call it?"

I could not escape the question. "They say it is the cry of the Hound of the Baskervilles."

He sighed deeply and was silent for a few moments.

At last he said, "My God, can these old tales be true? Is it possible that I am really in danger from a supernatural evil? You don't believe it, do you Watson?"

"No, no."

"Well, I laughed about it in London, but out here in the darkness on the moor, it's quite different. There was the footprint of the hound near my uncle's body. I don't think I'm easily frightened, Watson, but that sound really scared me."

"Shall we turn back?"

"No! We came to get our villain, and we shall do it. Come on!"

We moved slowly forward in the darkness. The tiny yellow light burned in front of us. At last we came to a group of rocks and saw the candle between them. Then we saw the criminal sitting on top of the rock. He didn't see us. He was an awful man to look at. He had the face of a hungry animal, with animal passions. His clothes, beard and hair were very dirty. His body was short and strong. His eyes moved back and forth like an animal who has heard the hunter.

Then he stood up, and I could read the fear on his face. Sir Henry and I jumped out from behind the rock. At that moment the criminal screamed, then turned and ran away over the rocks. We began to chase him but he was too fast. We watched him run in the moonlight until he disappeared in the distance.

Then a strange and unexpected thing occurred. We had turned to go home. The moon was low to the right. The tip of a rocky hill was between us and the moon. When I looked that way I clearly saw the figure of a tall man standing on the rock. His legs were slightly apart and his arms were folded on his chest. It was not the convict. I turned to tell the baronet but when I turned back, the man was gone. Another mystery on the moor.

Well, Holmes, today we plan to talk to the people at Princetown Prison and tell them what happened. It's just bad luck that we didn't catch him. I hope my reports are useful to you. It would be nice if you could come here yourself. I will write again soon.

Chapter 10
Parts of the Diary of Dr. Watson

October 16th. A dull and foggy day with some rain. The baronet is still upset after last night's excitement. My heart feels heavy with a sense of coming danger—a danger which I don't really understand.

But there are many good reasons to be afraid. There is the death of Sir Charles, just as in the ancient family tale. There are the reports by local people of a strange creature on the moor. Twice I have heard the sounds of a hound with my own ears. However, I will never believe that this is a supernatural devil dog. Perhaps there is a large dog living out there. But where could such a dog hide? Where would it find food? Why did no one see it in the daytime? And what about the people in this case? There was the man in the cab in London, the missing shoes, the letter warning Sir Henry against the moor. And who was that stranger on the rocks last night?

I know he is nobody I have seen who lives here. He was taller than Stapleton and thinner than Frankland. A stranger is following us, just as in London. I will do everything I can to find this man.

There was a problem this morning after breakfast. Barrymore asked to speak privately with Sir Henry. I heard loud voices several times as they talked in the study. A while later the baronet opened the door and called for me.

"Barrymore is upset," he said. "He thinks it was unfair for us to hunt his wife's brother after he told us his secret. And I think that this villain is a public danger. No one is safe until he is back in prison."

The butler was standing very pale but calmly before us.

"I can promise you he will never trouble anyone in this country again. Sir Henry, in a few days he will take a ship to South America. Please don't tell the police, sir. They have stopped looking for him there. He can wait quietly until the ship comes. He won't hurt anyone now."

"What do you think, Watson?"

"Well, if he were out of the country it would save us some tax money."

10. Parts of the Diary of Dr. Watson

"All right, Barrymore. We won't say anything," said Sir Henry.

"God bless you, sir, and thank you! My wife will be so happy."

Barrymore turned to go, but then he stopped and came back.

"You've been so kind to us, sir, that I would like to help you in return. I know something, Sir Henry, which I haven't told to anyone. It's about Sir Charles."

The baronet and I were both on our feet. "Do you know how he died?"

"No, sir, I don't know that."

"What then?"

"I know why he was at the moor gate at that hour. It was to meet a woman."

"To meet a woman! Him?"

"Yes, sir."

"And the woman's name?"

"I can't give you the name, sir, but I can tell you the letters of her name. They are L.L."

"How do you know this, Barrymore?"

"Well, Sir Henry, your uncle had a letter that morning. I noticed that it came from the village of Coombe Tracey, and was written by a woman."

"Well?"

"I forgot about it until my wife cleaned his

study a few weeks after he died. She found pieces of a burned letter in his fireplace. Everything was burned except one bit at the end of the page. It said: 'Please, please, as you are a gentleman, burn this letter, and be at the gate by ten o'clock.' Beneath it were signed the letters L.L."

"Do you know who L.L. is?"

"No, sir. But I think that lady could tell us a lot about Sir Charles's death."

"Why didn't you say anything before, Barrymore?"

"Well, sir, immediately after this is when we started to have our own problems with Selden. Also, we both liked Sir Charles very much and this seemed like a personal matter between him and a lady——"

"I understand. Thank you, Barrymore, you can go."

When the butler left us Sir Henry turned to me. "Well, Watson?"

"I will inform Holmes at once. This may be the clue he's looking for."

I went to my room and wrote the report of that morning to Holmes. I knew that he had been very busy lately with his other cases. I wished that he was here.

10. Parts of the Diary of Dr. Watson

October 17th. It rained all day today. I thought of the criminal out on the cold, wet moor. I'm sure he is suffering for his crimes.

Back on the road I met Dr. Mortimer who had come in his small wagon from Foulmire. He gave me a ride to the Hall. The man is very upset about his dog, a spaniel, which disappeared on the moor several days ago. I thought about that poor horse in the Grimpen Mire. I don't think he'll see his little dog again.

"By the way, Mortimer," I said, "does anyone live around here whom you don't know?"

"Hardly anyone."

"Can you think of a woman whose names begin with L.L.?"

He thought for a few minutes.

"No, I can't," he said. "Oh, wait a moment," he added. "There is Laura Lyons—her initials are L.L.—but she lives in Coombe Tracey."

"Who is she?" I asked.

"She is the daughter of that odd fellow, Frankland. She married an artist named Lyons. He wasn't a very honest man and later he left her. Her father didn't like the marriage and made life difficult for them."

"How does she live?"

"I think old Frankland gives her a little money,

but he hasn't got much more to give. Some people around here knew of her troubles and tried to help her. Stapleton for one, and Sir Charles for another. I myself gave a small amount to help her start a business."

Tomorrow morning I will go to Coombe Tracey to try and find this Mrs. Laura Lyons.

I have only one other thing to report on this stormy day. This is the talk I had with Barrymore when he brought me coffee in the library.

"Well," I said, "has your wife's brother departed, or is he still out on the moor?"

"I don't know, sir. I hope to God he is gone! I haven't heard from him since I left food for him three days ago."

"Did you see him then?"

"No, sir, but the food was gone when I went back."

"Then he was certainly there?"

"I suppose so, sir, unless it was the other man who took it."

I sat with my coffee cup halfway to my mouth and stared at him.

"There's another man on the moor?"

"Yes, sir, there is."

"Have you seen him?"

"No, sir."

10. Parts of the Diary of Dr. Watson

"How do you know about him then?"

"Selden told me about him more than a week ago. He's hiding too, but he's not a criminal. I don't like it, Dr. Watson. There's danger and evil out there." He spoke with true feeling.

"But what are you afraid of?"

"Look at Sir Charles's death! And the sounds on the moor! No local man would cross it after dark. Look at this stranger watching and waiting on the moor. What does it all mean? It means no good to the name of Baskerville. I'll be happy to leave here when the new housekeepers arrive."

"But what about this stranger," said I. "Where is he hiding, and what's he doing?"

"Selden saw him once or twice, but the stranger said nothing. He said the man seemed like a gentleman but doesn't know why he's there."

"Where does he live?"

"Among the ancient huts on the hillside."

"What about food?"

"Selden found out that he has a boy who works for him and brings all he needs from Coombe Tracey."

When the butler left I walked over to the window and looked into the blackness. I think the key to the mystery is there on the moor, and I will do all I can to find it.

Chapter 11
The Man on the Tor

The earlier chapter was taken from my diary up to October 18th when I learned two important things. The one, was that Mrs. Laura Lyons of Coombe Tracey arranged to see Sir Charles on the day and the hour of his death. The other was that the stranger on the moor was living in the ancient stone houses on the hillside.

The next morning Perkins drove me to Coombe Tracey. I had no trouble finding the lady's house. A maid showed me in. Mrs. Lyons was sitting in front of a typewriter. She was indeed beautiful. Her eyes and hair were the same rich, light brown color. She asked me what I wanted.

I didn't have a plan so I said, "I know your father."

It was not a good start.

"My father and I do not speak anymore," she

11. The Man on the Tor

said. "He didn't care about me. Other people like Sir Charles Baskerville kindly helped me."

"Actually, I came to see you about Sir Charles."

"What can I tell you about him?" she asked, a bit nervous.

"Did you write to him?"

The lady looked up quickly. "Why are you asking these questions?" she asked sharply.

"It is better that I talk to you in private than have others talk to you publicly."

She was silent and her face was pale. "Well, all right," she said. "Yes, I wrote to him once or twice to thank him."

"Do you have the dates of those letters?"

"No."

"Have you ever met him?"

"Yes, a couple times when he came into Coombe Tracey. He was a very shy, private man."

"But if you were not close friends then how did he know enough about your personal matters to help you?"

"There were several gentlemen who knew my sad history and helped me. One was Mr. Stapleton. He was very kind and he told Sir Charles about my problems."

"Did you ever write to Sir Charles asking him to meet you?" I continued.

Mrs. Lyons became slightly angry.

"Really, sir, this is a very personal question. The answer is no."

"Not on the very day of Sir Charles's death?"

The redness in her face became very white. Her dry lips could barely speak the word "No".

"Perhaps you've forgotten," said I. "I can tell you part of what you wrote. It said, 'Please, please, as you are a gentleman, burn this letter, and be at the gate by ten o'clock.'"

She looked shocked.

"I thought he was a gentleman!" her voice cried.

"That is not fair to Sir Charles. He did burn the letter. But sometimes it is possible to read them even when burned. Do you admit that you wrote that letter?"

"Yes, I wrote it!" she cried. "I won't deny it. I wanted to ask him for help. So I asked him to meet me."

"But why at that hour?"

"Because I had just learned he was going to London the next morning and might be gone for weeks and months. There were reasons I couldn't get there earlier."

"But why meet in the garden instead of in the house?"

11. The Man on the Tor

"Do you think a woman could go alone at that hour to a gentleman's house?"

"Well, what happened when you got there?"

"I never went."

"Mrs. Lyons!"

"No, I honestly never went."

"Why not?"

"It is a private matter. I cannot tell you."

"You admit that you asked to meet with Sir Charles at the very hour and place of his death, but you deny that you went there?"

"That is the truth."

Again and again I questioned her on that point, but her answer was always the same.

"Mrs. Lyons," I said, "I may have to go to the police if you don't tell me everything. Why did you deny writing to Sir Charles on that date?"

"Because I was afraid that I might be falsely blamed."

"And why was it so important for him to destroy the letter?"

"You read the letter so you know why."

"I did not say that I had read all the letter. That was only the last line or two. The letter had been burned and most of it was impossible to read. Again, why was it so important to destroy this letter?"

"I will tell you, then. Perhaps you already know

that I made a bad decision to marry, and am very sorry for it."

"I had heard that."

"My life has been a continuous problem with a husband I hate. The law is on his side, and I may be forced to live with him. In order to be free of him and be happy again I had to pay certain expenses. I knew Sir Charles was a generous man, and that he might help me if I told him my story."

"Then why didn't you go to see him?"

"Because someone else helped me in the meantime. I was going to write and tell him until I read about his death the next morning."

The woman's story seemed to fit. I believe she did not go to Baskerville Hall. I had a feeling, however, that she wasn't telling me everything.

Driving back to the Hall in the carriage I saw hill after hill with hundreds of ancient huts. Barrymore told me that the stranger lived in one of them. I planned to start looking on Black Tor, the place where I saw him standing that night. I was going to search until I found him.

Our bad luck in this case was beginning to change for the good. We passed the home of Mr. Frankland who was standing by the road.

"Good day, Dr. Watson," he cried with good cheer. "Give your horses a rest and come have a

11. The Man on the Tor

glass of wine with me."

My feelings towards him were not very friendly after what his daughter had told me. But I sent Perkins and the carriage ahead with a message to Sir Henry that I would walk home in time for dinner. Then I followed the white-haired, red-faced man into his dining room.

"This is one of the better days of my life," he said laughing. "I have won a double victory in court. One for the rights of the common man against the rich; the other to protect our public parks from the dirty people of Fernworthy."

"What do you gain by winning these court cases, Mr. Frankland?"

"Nothing, sir, nothing. I am proud to say that I act only from a sense of public duty. Although I'm sure that the people in Fernworthy will be angry with me tonight. Last time, they made a wooden figure of me and burned it in public. I'm also angry with the police for not protecting me better. I don't think I'll tell them that I know something very important."

"How do you mean?" I asked.

"It's about that criminal on the moor."

"You mean you know where he is?" said I.

"No, not exactly. But I'm quite sure I could lead the police to him if I wanted. The best way to catch that man is to find out where his food is, and follow him."

He was getting uncomfortably close to the truth. "Perhaps," said I, "but what makes you think he's on the moor?"

"Because I have seen a messenger bring him food."

Poor Barrymore! This nosy old man could bring serious trouble to the butler. However, his next remark made me feel better.

"Surprisingly, the messenger is a child. I see him every day through my telescope up on the roof. He passes along the same path at the same hour. He must be going to the criminal!"

What luck! A child! Barrymore said that our mystery man was helped by a boy. So it was the stranger, not the criminal, that Frankland knew of. I needed to find out what else he knew.

"Are you sure it's not a farmer's son taking dinner to his father?"

"Indeed, sir!" said the old man with fight in his eyes. "Do you see the hill beyond Black Tor over there? It is the rockiest part of the whole moor. There are no farms or animals there."

I admitted I was wrong. This seemed to please him and he was happy to continue.

"I've seen the boy again and again with his

11. The Man on the Tor

package. Every day, and sometimes twice a day. I am able—wait a moment, Dr. Watson. Do you also see something moving on that hillside?"

It was several miles off, but I could see a small dark dot against the dull green.

"Come!" cried Frankland, running upstairs. "You will see with your own eyes."

The telescope was a large and expensive one standing on three legs. Frankland looked through it and smiled.

"Quick, Watson, quick, before he passes over the hill!"

There he was, a small boy carrying a little package over his shoulder. I could see he was dressed in dirty clothes. When he got to the top he looked around carefully, then disappeared over the hill.

"Well! Am I right?"

"Certainly, there is a boy who seems to have some secret duty."

"Even our foolish police chief could guess what that duty is. But I will tell them nothing, Dr. Watson, and you won't either. Not a word!"

"Just as you wish."

"Those police have treated me shamefully. They don't care about me one bit. When the facts of my next case come out in court the rest of the county will take my side. Surely you are not going, Dr.

Watson? Won't you help me finish the rest of this wine in honor of this occasion?"

But I was able to excuse myself and said goodbye. I stayed on the road until I was away from the old man's sight, then I turned and crossed the moor. I felt very lucky.

The sun was already setting when I reached the hilltop. There was no sound and no movement except for one bird high above. He and I were the only living things between heaven and earth. I couldn't see the boy anywhere. But I looked down the hill into a group of stone huts and I saw one that still had a roof. This must be where the stranger is hiding.

I walked slowly up to the hut, as Stapleton would do when chasing an insect with his net. I could see a tiny path that led to the door and I knew the house was being used by someone. All was silent inside. The stranger might be in there, or he might be outside. I could feel my nerves shaking from the adventure. I threw down my cigarette, put my hand on my gun, and walked quickly to the door. I opened it, but the place was empty.

However, someone was using the house. The ashes of a fire were on the ground. Beside it was a bowl for cooking and some water. There were several empty metal cans nearby, and a half bottle

11. The Man on the Tor

of wine. There were also blankets and a raincoat. I could see the cloth bag the boy had brought containing some bread, meat and fruit. Then I saw a sheet of paper with writing on it and my heart jumped. I raised it to my eyes and read: "Dr. Watson has gone to Coombe Tracey."

So it was I, and not Sir Henry, who was being followed by this mystery man. Perhaps I was being watched at this same moment.

I searched around the hut for more information but found none. Nor could I find any clues about the man who lived here. It was clear that he needed very little and didn't care much about comfort. Was he our evil enemy or our protecting friend? I decided to find out. I sat in the darkest corner of the little hut and waited.

Then at last I heard him. Far away came the sharp sound of a shoe against a stone. Then another, nearer and nearer. I took out my gun and held it tightly. I was ready to shoot. There was a moment of silence as he stopped outside the house. Then he took two more steps and a shadow fell across the door.

"It is a lovely evening, my dear Watson," said a well-known voice. "I really think that you will enjoy the view from out here."

Chapter 12
Death on the Moor

For a moment or two I sat in shock, unable to believe my ears. At the same time I felt a huge relief. That voice could only belong to one person in the world.

"Holmes!" I cried—"Holmes!"

"Come out," he said, "and please be careful with the gun."

I walked out under the short door and there he sat sitting on a stone. His eyes were dancing with enjoyment as he looked at me. He was thin and tired, but looked clean and healthy. His face was browned from the sun.

"I'm so happy to see you," I said as I shook his hand.

"And surprised?"

"Very."

"The surprise was not just yours. I had no idea that you had found my little country house until I

12. Death on the Moor

was just a few steps from the door."

"My footprints?"

"No, Watson, your tobacco. I saw the end of a cigarette marked Bradley, Oxford Street, next to the path. I knew that you were nearby. And knowing you as well as I do I was sure you were inside waiting for me with your gun. Did you think that I was the criminal?"

"I didn't know who you were but I was certain to find out."

"Excellent, Watson! And how did you find me? Was it that night you went looking for the criminal, when I foolishly stood in front of the moon?"

"Yes, I saw you then. And today I saw your boy coming here so I knew where to look."

"Ha! I see that Cartwright has brought up some supplies. What's this paper? It says you've been to Coombe Tracey?"

"Yes."

"To see Mrs. Laura Lyons?"

"Exactly."

"Well done! Our detective work has been very similar. I'm sure that when we compare our results we shall uncover this mystery."

"Well, I am very, very glad that you are here, for my nerves were becoming rather weak. But how did you get here, and what have you been doing? I thought that you were in Baker Street working on another case?"

"That is what I wanted you to think."

"Then you used me, and you do not trust me!" I cried with just a bit of anger.

"My dear fellow, you are always of very great value to me. Please forgive me if you are feeling tricked. Honestly, it was necessary for the case that you come here alone. It was important that our enemies didn't know I was here."

"But why not tell me you were here?"

"Because I might have been discovered if you tried to help me. That's why I brought Cartwright with me. He brings me food and clean clothes. My needs are simple. He also gives me an extra pair of eyes and feet."

"Then my reports have all been wasted!" I said with hurt feelings.

Holmes took a pile of papers from his pocket.

"Here are your reports, my friend. I've read all of them more than once. I arranged with the mails to receive them one day later. You've done an excellent job."

Holmes's kind words removed the anger from my mind.

"And now, Watson, tell me about your visit to Mrs. Lyons."

12. Death on the Moor

It had become cool and dark so we went into the hut. I told Holmes of my talk with the lady. He was very interested in every word.

"This is most important," he said when I had finished. "It makes the situation much clearer. Did you know that this lady and Mr. Stapleton have very close relations?"

"I had no idea."

"There can be no doubt. They meet, they write, there is a complete understanding between them. Now, this puts a powerful piece of information in our hands. If I could only use it to separate his wife—— "

"His wife?"

"Yes, Watson. The lady who you know as Beryl Stapleton is really his wife, not his sister."

"My God, Holmes! Are you sure of that? How could he allow Sir Henry to fall in love with her?"

"Sir Henry's falling in love will only hurt Sir Henry."

"But why this trick?"

"Because he knew that she would be much more useful to him in the character of a free woman."

Suddenly I had a terrible feeling about that naturalist with his insect net. Stapleton was a man of great patience with a smiling face and a murderous heart.

"Then he is our enemy—he followed us in London?"

"I believe so."

"And the warning—it must have come from her?"

"Exactly."

Now I began to see the evil which I had only guessed at before.

"How can you be sure Holmes that the woman is his wife?"

"Because he told you that he was once a schoolmaster in the north of England. There are very good records on schools and it is easy to find former teachers and masters. I found out that there was a school in the north that had closed in very bad circumstances, and that the man who owned it had disappeared with his wife. His name was different then, but you described the same man, especially his interest in insects."

The darkness was rising from the shadows.

"If this woman is really his wife, then what about Mrs. Laura Lyons?" I asked.

"Your talk with the lady has helped me. I did not know that she planned to leave her husband. She thought Stapleton was unmarried and hoped to become his wife."

"And when she learns the truth?"

12. Death on the Moor

"Why, then she may be of service to us. We must both go visit her tomorrow. Don't you think, Watson, that it's time for you to return to the Hall?"

All the color in the sky was gone, and a few stars were shining.

"One last question, Holmes," I said as I got up. "What does he want?"

Holmes's voice sank as he answered.

"It is murder, Watson — cold-blooded, terrible murder. One more day, perhaps two, and he will be our prisoner. The danger is that he will strike at Sir Henry first. You must protect Sir Henry as a mother protects her child. What's that?"

A long, terrible scream broke the silence of the moor. My blood turned to ice.

"Oh, my God!" I cried. "What is it?"

Holmes had jumped to his feet, and I saw his dark, thin figure at the door of the hut. His head was leaning forward into the darkness.

"Sshh!" he whispered. "Sshh!"

The cry had been loud, but from a distant place. Now it seemed nearer, louder.

"Where is it, Watson?" Holmes whispered. I knew from the tone of his voice that my strong friend was shaken to the soul.

"There, I think." I pointed into the darkness.

"No, there!"

The scream came again, even louder and nearer. And a new sound mixed with it. A deep roar, like the low sound of the sea.

"The hound!" cried Holmes. "Come, Watson, come! God, I hope we're not too late!"

He started running at top speed over the moor, and I followed. We heard one last cry of despair, and then a dull heavy hitting sound. We stopped to listen. There was no wind, only silence.

I saw Holmes put his hand to his head like a man in pain. He kicked his foot into the ground.

"He has beaten us, Watson. We are too late."

"No, no, surely not!"

"I was a fool to wait so long. And you, Watson, see what happens when you forget your duties! But, by Heaven, we will get him!"

We ran blindly through the night, pushing through plants and bushes, up and down the hills. At every rise we stopped to look around, but it was dark and nothing moved.

Finally, Holmes cried, "Look, what's that?"

We heard a very low murmuring sound to the left. There was a group of pointed rocks where the hill suddenly dropped off. We could see a body among the rocks below, and ran towards it. It was a man lying face down on the rocks his head bent under him in a terrible curl. Now there was only si-

12. Death on the Moor

lence. Holmes struck a match. The dead man's head was crushed. Blood flowed into the ground. And in the light we saw something else which made our hearts sick—the body of Sir Henry Baskerville!

He wore the same wool suit which he had when he first came to Baker Street. We saw it clearly and then the match died, as the hope went out of our souls. Holmes made a painful sound and his face was terribly white.

"That devil! That devil!" I cried in pain and anger. "Oh, Holmes, I shall never forgive myself for leaving him to this fate."

"I am more to blame than you, Watson. In order to complete my case I have killed the man I tried to help. It is the greatest blow of my working life. But why did he come alone out here on the moor?"

"Oh God, we heard his terrible screams but we couldn't save him! Where is this hound which chased him to his death? It may be around here now. And Stapleton, where is he? He shall pay for this tragedy."

"He will, Watson. I will make sure of that. Uncle and nephew have been murdered. The one frightened to death by the sight of the beast, the other killed trying to run from it. But now we must prove that there really is a beast. Sir Henry died from the fall. We have no evidence of an animal.

Stapleton may be clever but he will be in my power by tomorrow!"

We stood with shocked, saddened hearts on either side of the body. The moon rose and we climbed to the rocks from where our poor friend had fallen. Across the moor was a single light coming from the lonely Stapleton house. I cursed it.

"Why don't we get him right now?"

"Our case is not complete. The fellow is intelligent and clever. We must first prove the facts. If we make one mistake he might escape."

"What can we do?"

"We must wait for tomorrow. Tonight we can only see to our poor friend."

We went back down the steep hill to the body. It was a truly painful sight. My eyes filled with tears.

"Good heavens, Holmes, are you crazy?"

My friend was suddenly dancing and laughing and shaking my hand. I didn't understand.

"A beard! The man has a beard! It is not the baronet—my God, it is my neighbor, the criminal!"

We quickly turned over the body. It was the bloody face of Selden, the criminal.

Instantly, I remembered the baronet had given some of his old clothes to Barrymore as a gift when his new clothes arrived. Barrymore had then given some to Selden. Shoes, shirt, coat, hat—they were

12. Death on the Moor

all Sir Henry's. This was still a tragedy, but this man deserved to die. My heart jumped with joy and thanks.

"Then it was the clothes that killed this poor devil," he said. "The hound was trained to follow a piece of Sir Henry's clothing—probably that shoe taken from the hotel. But how did Selden, in the darkness, know that the hound was after him?"

"He heard him."

"I don't think that would make a hard man like this scream wildly for help. He probably ran a long way after he knew the animal was following him. How did he know?"

"Well, what shall we do with the poor man's body?" I asked.

"Let's carry it to one of the stone huts until we can talk to the police. Look, Watson, what do I see? Oh my, it's our man himself, walking this way! Wonderful. Say nothing to make him suspect us."

A figure was approaching us in the moonlight. He stopped briefly when he saw us.

"Why, Dr. Watson, is that you? I certainly didn't expect to see you out here at this time of night. But, dear me, what's this? Is somebody hurt? Not—oh no, is it our friend Sir Henry?" He ran past me and bent down to look at the dead man. I heard a shocked sound in his throat.

"Who—who's this?" his voice shook.

"It is Selden, the man who escaped from Princetown."

Stapleton turned a sick color. But with great effort he was able to control his shock and disappointment. He looked at us.

"Dear me! What a terrible affair! How did he die?"

"He appears to have broken his neck after falling onto these rocks. My friend and I were taking a walk on the moor when we heard a cry."

"I heard a cry also. That's why I came out. I was uneasy about Sir Henry."

"Why?" I asked.

"Because I asked him to come to our house for a visit. When he did not come I was surprised. I worried about his safety when I heard screams on the moor. By the way," his eyes moved back and forth from Holmes to me, "did you hear anything else besides a cry?"

"No," said Holmes, "did you?"

"No."

"What do you mean, then?"

"Oh, you know the stories that the country people tell about a devil hound at night upon the moor."

"We heard nothing of the kind," I said.

12. Death on the Moor

"How do you think this poor fellow died?"

"I believe that the man's bad mental and physical condition made him crazy. He ran around the moor in a wild manner and fell over here, breaking his neck."

"That seems reasonable," said Stapleton, as he breathed easier. "What do you think about it, Mr. Sherlock Holmes?"

"Ah, you know my name," he said.

"We have been expecting you around here since Dr. Watson came down. You are in time to see a tragedy."

"Yes, indeed. I'm sure that my friend is correct about what happened here. I will take an unpleasant memory back to London with me tomorrow."

"Oh, you return tomorrow?"

"That is my plan."

"I hope your visit has shined some light on those mysteries which have puzzled us."

Holmes lifted his shoulders.

"One cannot always be successful. A detective needs facts, not ancient stories. It has not been a very satisfying case."

My friend spoke in a direct and unconcerned manner. Stapleton still gave him a hard look. Then he turned to me.

"I think that if we cover his face he'll be safe

until morning."

And that's what we did. Holmes and I set off to Baskerville Hall, and the naturalist returned alone. Looking back we saw him walking slowly away over the moor. Behind him lay that small black spot where the man's life came to a terrible end.

Chapter 13
Fixing the Nets

"We've almost got him," said Holmes as we walked together across the moor. "What nerve that fellow has! Did you see how quickly he recovered from the shock of finding he had murdered the wrong man? I tell you again, Watson, this man is dangerous."

"I'm sorry that he saw you, Holmes."

"Me too. But it can't be avoided."

"Do you think he will change his plans knowing that you're here now?"

"Perhaps. Most clever criminals believe they are too intelligent to get caught."

"Why shouldn't we take him to the police right now?"

"My dear Watson, you are certainly a man of action. However, you must understand that we have to prove he is guilty in court. At the moment we can prove nothing, mainly because he is using a dog."

"What about Sir Charles's death?"

"Found dead without a mark on his body. Where is the evidence of a hound? Where are the marks of his bite?"

"Well, what about tonight?"

"Same situation. There is no direct relation between the hound and the man's death. We never saw the hound. We heard it, but we can't prove that it was chasing this man. No, my friend, we have no case yet, but we will."

"How do you plan to do that?"

"I have great hopes that Mrs. Laura Lyons will help us when we tell her the truth. Tomorrow will be an important day for us."

He said nothing else, and walked in thought to the Baskerville gates.

"Are you coming in?"

"Yes, I see no further reason to hide. But, Watson, say nothing of the hound to Sir Henry. Let him think that Selden's death was an accident. He will need his nerve when he goes to the Stapleton house tomorrow for dinner."

"I am dining with him there."

"Then you must excuse yourself and he must go alone. We can easily arrange that. Now, shall we go in and eat?"

Sir Henry was very surprised and pleased to see

13. Fixing the Nets

Sherlock Holmes. During our late dinner we told the baronet as much about our experience as we thought he should know. But first it was my duty to tell Barrymore and his wife about Selden. She cried. To everyone else he was an evil man, but to her he would always be her sweet little brother.

"I've been here alone in the house all day since Watson left this morning," said the baronet. "In fact, Stapleton invited me to dinner but I had promised Watson I wouldn't leave the house alone, so I didn't go."

"By the way," said Holmes, "you might want to know that we have been crying over your broken neck?"

Sir Henry opened his eyes, "How do you mean?"

"The poor criminal was dressed in your clothes. Barrymore may get into trouble with the police for that."

"That's unlikely. There was no mark on any of them, I'm sure."

"That's lucky for Barrymore—in fact, it's lucky for all of you, since you are all on the wrong side of the law in this matter. As a good detective perhaps I should take you all into the police."

"But how about the case?" asked the baronet. "Watson and I have learned some things, but not enough. Have you uncovered this great mystery?"

"It has been a very difficult case, but I think it will soon be finished."

"Watson probably told you we heard the hound on the moor. I'm sure there is some creature out there. If you can find that animal then I'll say you are the world's greatest detective."

"With your help I think I can do that."

"Tell me what to do and I'll do it."

"Very good; and you must do exactly as I say. I think——"

Holmes stopped suddenly and stared over my head into the air.

"What is it?" we both cried.

When he looked down at us I could see an excitement in his eyes. "I love portraits," he said pointing towards the wall, "and you have some fine ones. I'll bet that lady in the blue dress was painted by Kneller. And the gentleman with white hair was painted by Reynolds. Are they all family portraits?"

"Every one."

"Who is the gentleman with the telescope?"

"That is Admiral Baskerville, who served in the West Indies. The man with the blue coat is Sir William Baskerville, who was in the House of Commons."

"And this man on the horse?"

13. Fixing the Nets

"Ah, he is the cause of our problems. That's Hugo, the one who started the Hound of the Baskervilles. That was painted in 1647."

I looked with interest at the portrait.

"Dear me!" said Holmes, "he looks like a quiet, weak man. I had imagined him as a stronger, more powerful person. But I can see a bit of the devil in those eyes."

Holmes said little more, but the picture of the old Baskerville clearly interested him. He often looked at it during the meal. Later, when Sir Henry had gone to his room, he took me back to the dining room. He held a candle up to the portrait.

"Do you see anything there?"

I looked at the broad hat with feather, at the curly hair, the white silk shirt, and the straight, serious face. He was not ugly or handsome, just hard and firm of character.

"Is it like anyone you know?"

"Well, his mouth is like Sir Henry's."

"Wait a moment!" He then stood on a chair and with his arm he covered the hat and other clothes so that I could see only the face.

"Good heavens!" I cried in surprise.

The face of Stapleton jumped out of the portrait.

"Ha, now you see it. My detective eyes are trained to examine faces."

"They almost look the same."

"Yes, it is unbelievably similar, both physically and in spirit. Stapleton is a Baskerville, I'm sure."

"Do you think he wants to become the baronet?"

"Exactly. This good bit of luck is an important missing piece of the puzzle. We have him, Watson, we have him. Tomorrow night he will be in our net just like one of his insects. Then we will put him in our Baker Street collection!" Holmes then burst into great laughter.

I woke up at my usual hour in the morning, but Holmes was already outside.

"Yes, we have a full day today," he remarked and he rubbed his hands with joy. "The nets are in place, and now we begin to pull them in."

"Have you been on the moor already?"

"I have sent a message from Grimpen to Princetown as to the death of Selden. I can promise that none of you will be troubled by the police. I also sent word to my faithful boy, Cartwright."

"What is the next move?"

"To see Sir Henry. Ah, here he is!"

"Good morning, Holmes," said the baronet. "You look like a general who is planning a battle."

"That is the exact situation. Watson was asking for orders."

13. Fixing the Nets

"And so do I."

"Very good. I understand that you are dining with the Stapletons tonight?"

"I hope that you will also come. They are very nice people and would be happy to see you."

"I'm afraid that Watson and I must go to London. I think we can be more useful there than here at this moment."

"To London?" The baronet seemed disappointed. "I hoped that you would stay here with me. This is not a very pleasant place when one is alone."

"My dear fellow, you gave me your word that you would do what I told you. Now you must trust me. Please tell your friends that we would like to see them, but we have immediate business in London. We hope to return to Devonshire very soon."

"If you insist."

"There is no choice, I promise you."

The baronet looked hurt by our leaving him.

"When do you desire to go?" he asked coldly.

"Immediately after breakfast. We will drive to Coombe Tracey. Watson, you will send a note to Stapleton to tell him you're sorry you can't come."

"Sir Henry, this evening I want you to drive to Merripit House. Then send back your carriage, and tell them that you intend to walk home."

"To walk across the moor?"

"Yes."

"But that is what you have always told me not to do."

"This time you may do it with safety. I trust your nerve and bravery. It's important that you do this."

"Then I will do it."

"And please stay on the path that goes straight from Merripit House to the Grimpen Road. It is your usual way home."

"I will do just what you say."

"Very good. I would like to get away right after breakfast and reach London in the afternoon."

I was very much surprised by this program. I could only obey Holmes, however, so we said good-bye to our sad friend. Two hours later we were at the station of Coombe Tracey. A small boy was standing at the station.

"Any orders, sir?"

"You will take this train to London, Cartwright. The moment you arrive you will send a wire to Sir Henry Baskerville, in my name. Tell him that if he finds the pocketbook which I have dropped he is to send it by registered post to Baker Street."

"Yes, sir."

"And ask at the station office if there is a message for me."

The boy returned with a telegram, which Holmes

13. Fixing the Nets

handed to me. It ran:

> Wire received. Coming down with unsigned police papers. Arrive five-forty.
>
> LESTRADE.

"He is a very good police detective, and we may need his help. Now, Watson, I think that we should visit Mrs. Laura Lyons."

Holmes's plan was becoming clear. He would use the baronet to assure the Stapletons that we were really gone. Then we would return when we were really needed. The telegram from London, if Sir Henry mentioned it to the Stapletons would remove the last doubt from their minds. Already I could feel our nets drawing closer.

Mrs. Laura Lyons was in her office. Sherlock Holmes was very direct with her.

"I am examining the circumstances of the death of Sir Charles Baskerville," said he. "Yesterday you spoke with Dr. Watson. You admit that you asked Sir Charles to be at the gate at ten o'clock. We know that was the place and hour of his death. You have not told us about the relation between these events."

"There is no relation."

"In that case the timing is quite unbelievable.

However, I think we shall prove that there was a relation. I wish to be perfectly honest with you, Mrs. Lyons. We regard this case as murder. The evidence may point to your friend Mr. Stapleton and his wife."

The lady jumped from her chair.

"His wife!" she cried.

"The fact is no longer a secret. The person who has passed for his sister is really his wife."

Mrs. Lyons sat back down. Her hands were holding tightly on to the chair. Her fingers were turning white from the force.

"His wife!" she said again. "His wife! He is not a married man."

Sherlock Holmes lifted his shoulders.

"Prove it to me! Prove it to me! And if you can——!" The flash of her eyes said more than any words.

"I am prepared to do that," said Holmes, taking several papers from his pocket. "Here is a photograph of the couple taken in York four years ago. It is written 'Mr. and Mrs. Vandeleur,' but you will easily recognize him, and perhaps her also. Here are three witnesses who described Mr. and Mrs. Vandeleur when they owned St. Oliver's private school. Read them and see if you can doubt who these people are."

13. Fixing the Nets

She glanced at them, then looked up at us with the face of a woman in despair.

"Mr. Holmes," she said, "this man has offered to marry me on the condition that I get a lawful separation from my husband. He has never told me the truth, only lies. I thought he loved and wanted me, but he only used me. He is an evil man. I feel hurt and dishonored. I will tell you anything you like. But please believe that I never dreamed of harming that dear old gentleman, Sir Charles. He was a kind friend."

"I believe you, madam," said Sherlock Holmes. "This must be very painful for you. The sending of this letter to Sir Charles was Stapleton's idea?"

"He told me what to write."

"And he told you that you could receive help for your separation expenses from Sir Charles?"

"Exactly. Later he changed his mind about asking another man to help me. He said that somehow he would help me himself. Then he told me not to keep the appointment. The next day I read the reports of the death in the newspaper. He made me promise to say nothing about my appointment with Sir Charles. I did what he told me because I loved him."

"I think that you are very lucky to be alive," said Sherlock Holmes. "We must say good-bye now, Mrs.

Lyons. You will probably hear from us again very soon."

Later that afternoon the London train arrived at the station. We greeted Lestrade. He was a small but powerful looking man. He and Holmes had known each other many years.

"Ah, the country air feels fresh," he said. "What's the plan?"

"We have two hours before we need to start," said Holmes. "Let's get some dinner, shall we?"

Chapter 14
The Hound of the Baskervilles

Sherlock Holmes never told anyone else his full plans until a case was finished. He liked to be in control and to surprise others. As we rode the carriage in the cold night air I could only guess at our plan of action. Finally we arrived near the path to Merripit House. We started walking.

"Do you have a gun, Lestrade?"

"Always," said the little detective smiling. "Tell me, Holmes, what do we do now?"

"That light ahead is Merripit House. We'll walk very quietly towards it then we'll wait."

We stopped about two hundred yards from the house.

"This is close enough," he said. "We will hide among these rocks. Watson, you know the house. Move forward very quietly and see what they are doing inside."

I stood behind the low wall next to the fruit trees and looked straight into the window.

Stapleton and Sir Henry were in the room but Miss Stapleton was not. They were smoking cigars, and drinking wine. Stapleton was talking in a lively manner, but the baronet did not look very happy.

As I watched them Stapleton got up and left the room. I heard the sound of a door opening and shoes walking on a path. I saw the naturalist walk to a small gardenhouse and unlock the door. Something moved inside as he entered it. A minute later he locked the door and went back to the house to rejoin Sir Henry. I walked quietly back to my companions and told them what I had seen.

"It's very strange that the lady is not there. I wonder where she is," Holmes said.

Above the great Grimpen Mire there was a thick, white fog. The moon was shining on it. It looked like an ice field. Holmes was looking at it.

"It's moving toward us, Watson."

"Is that serious?"

"Very serious. It is the one and only thing which could hurt my plans. I hope Sir Henry leaves soon before the fog gets here."

Every minute we waited brought the fog in closer and closer. As we watched, it slowly surrounded the house. Holmes was worried and impatient.

"If he isn't out in fifteen minutes the path will be covered and we won't be able to see anything."

Gradually the fog flowed forward and covered us. We could only see a short distance.

Holmes suddenly dropped to his knees and put his ear to the ground. "Thank God, I think I hear him coming."

There was a sound of quick steps along the path. The steps grew louder. Then we saw Sir Henry walk by in the fog. He looked back nervously. He didn't see us behind the rocks.

"Psst!" cried Holmes, as he took out his gun. "Look out! It's coming!"

There was the sound of a running animal. All three of us stared into the fog. Suddenly we saw something very shocking. It was a hound, a huge dark-black creature, like nothing I'd ever seen before. Fire came from its open mouth, its eyes glowed with light, and flames seemed to come from its body. It looked like the devil himself. For a moment we were all too frightened to move. Then Holmes and I both fired our guns. The creature gave a terrible cry. However, it continued forward after Sir Henry.

But the animal's cry of pain gave us hope. If he was hurt then he was not supernatural. We could kill him. We ran after the hound as fast as we could.

In front of us on the path we heard screams of fear from Sir Henry. Then the hound roared and leaped at the baronet, knocking him to the ground, and going for the throat. At that same instant Holmes fired five shots from his gun into the side of the beast. With a last scream of pain it rolled onto its back, all four feet moving crazily. Then it stopped moving. The giant hound was dead.

Sir Henry was laying on the ground. He was not hurt, but he was in shock. Lestrade put a small bottle of whiskey between the baronet's teeth. Two frightened eyes looked up at us.

"My God!" he whispered. "What was it?"

"It's dead, whatever it is," said Holmes.

The terrible creature was the largest, strongest dog we'd ever seen. It was dead but a blue flame came from its mouth and eyes. I placed my hand on the mouth and my fingers also glowed in the darkness.

"The substance is called phosphorous," I said.

"A very clever, very evil idea," said Holmes, looking at the hound. "Sir Henry, we are very, very sorry that this happened to you. I never expected a creature like this."

"You've saved my life."

"But we almost killed you first. How are you feeling?"

"Oh, I think I'll be all right. What do you plan to do now?"

"To leave you here. You are not ready for another adventure tonight."

He tried to stand on his feet, but it was difficult. We helped him to a rock where he sat shaking, his face in his hands.

"We must leave you now for a short while," said Holmes, "and find our man."

We began walking back along the path. "I'm sure he's not in the house. He probably followed the hound but ran away when he heard the shots." The front door was open, so we ran into the house. The old servant was quite surprised to see us. We looked in every corner, but saw no sign of Stapleton. On the upper floor, however, one of the bedroom doors was locked.

"There's someone in here," cried Lestrade. "I can hear a movement. Open this door!"

Holmes kicked the door with his foot just above the lock and it flew open. We did not find the cruel and clever Stapleton, but we were greatly surprised.

The room was where Stapleton kept his insect collections. In the center of the room was a wooden pole used to support the old roof. There was a person tied to this pole and covered in sheets so that we could not tell who it was. We began to remove the sheets from around the face and neck. Seconds later we were looking into the dark, sad, fearful eyes of Mrs. Stapleton. At that moment her beautiful head fell upon her chest. She had fainted. I saw the clear red mark on her neck where she had been beaten.

"The devil!" cried Holmes. "Lestrade, give me your whiskey bottle!"

She opened her eyes again a moment later.

"Is he safe?" she asked. "Did he escape?"

"He cannot escape from us, madam."

"No, no. I did not mean my husband. Sir Henry? Is he safe?"

"Yes."

"And the hound?"

"It is dead."

She gave a long grateful sigh.

"Thank God! Oh, this villain! See how he treated me!" She showed us her arms which were covered with marks from being beaten. "But this is nothing, nothing! It is my mind and soul that he has destroyed. Now I know that I have only been used and fooled by him. He never really loved me." She began to cry passionately.

"You have good reason to hate him, madam," said Holmes. "Tell us where he is."

"There is only one place where he can run," she answered. "There is an old mine on an island in the heart of the mire. That's where he kept his hound. It's also his hiding place. I'm sure he's there."

The fog lay like white cotton against the window. Holmes held the light towards it.

"See," said he. "No one could find his way into the Grimpen Mire tonight."

"He may find his way in, but never out," she cried happily. "We marked the path to the mine with guiding sticks. He won't be able to see them."

We knew that we couldn't follow him in this fog. Meanwhile we left Lestrade to guard the house while Holmes and I went back with the baronet to Baskerville Hall. We had to tell him the shocking truth about the Stapletons, and the woman he loved. The night's adventures had broken his nerve. By morning he was in bed sick with a fever under the care of Dr. Mortimer. The two of them later traveled around the world together so that Sir Henry could fully recover his health.

And now I quickly come to the end of this most unusual case. Mrs. Stapleton took us to the path through the mire the next morning. The fog had lifted. She now hated her husband and was eager to help us. We followed the dry-land marker sticks through the wet, dangerous mire. The water and plants had a strong smell. Once or twice we took a wrong step and our legs sank into the mire. Then we spotted a dark object near the path and picked it up. It was Sir Henry's old black shoe.

"Well," said Holmes, "Stapleton probably first let the hound smell the shoe, then he dropped it here as he ran away from us. At least we know that he safely came this far."

But we would never know more than that. There were no footprints in that terrible place. Only the earth itself knows what happened to Stapleton in the fog last night. We believe that the body of that cruel man lies at the bottom of Grimpen Mire.

We found the old mine and the place where he kept his hound. There was a dog chain and a pile of bones. There were also the remains of what looked like a little brown animal.

"A dog!" said Holmes. "By God, I believe the hound ate poor Mortimer's little spaniel. Well, I don't know if this place has any more secrets for us. Stapleton could hide his hound, but not its voice. He wanted to create a hell-hound from the ancient Baskerville family story. Here is the can of phosphorous mix he used. It certainly frightened old Sir Charles to death; the escaped criminal too. It also stopped the farmers and country people from walking on the moor and asking questions. Very clever, indeed. I said it in London, Watson, and I say it again now. This is the most dangerous man we have ever hunted down. And now he lies there in the green mire."

Chapter 15
Looking Back

It was the end of November. Holmes and I sat in front of a warm fire in our Baker Street sitting room. Since returning from Devonshire he had been busy, and successful, with other important cases. He was in a good mood. Sir Henry and Dr. Mortimer were in London on their way to the sea voyage to restore the baronet's health. They visited us earlier at Baker Street. I asked my friend to talk about the case.

"Sometimes when my mind is fixed on one case it is easy to forget the details of another," said Holmes. "But I'll try to remember what I can. I have had two long talks with Mrs. Stapleton and I now believe that every question has been cleared up. I learned that Stapleton was the son of Rodger Baskerville who was Sir Charles's younger brother. Rodger got into trouble and escaped to South America where they said he died unmarried. He did, however, marry

15. Looking Back

and have one child. This child later married Beryl Garcia, a Costa Rican beauty. He stole a lot of public money, then left for England. He changed his name to Vandeleur and opened a school in Yorkshire. He hoped to make money but the school failed badly. Then they changed their name to Stapleton and moved to the south of England.

"Now we come to the interesting part. The fellow knew that there were only two people keeping him from becoming a rich baronet. He badly wanted the ancient family manor and would do anything to get it. He decided to use his wife in the character of his sister. Then he found a place to live near Baskerville Hall. There he began a friendship with Sir Charles Baskerville and the neighbors. Stapleton learned about the family hound, and about Sir Charles's weak heart. Then he made a plan to kill the baronet.

"And the plan worked perfectly. He bought the strongest and most deadly hound he could find. He decided to hide it in Grimpen Mire, which he knew very well from his insect hunts. His idea to put a phosphorous substance on the hound was especially clever and evil. He then waited for his chance.

"It took a long time because the old gentleman never wanted to leave the manor grounds at night. Later he had an opportunity because of Mrs. Laura

Lyons. She thought he was a single man and had fallen in love with him. He promised her that he would marry her if she could get a divorce from her husband. Then he learned that Sir Charles was about to leave for London. He had to act quickly. That's when he told Mrs. Lyons to write the letter to the old man asking to talk with him. He then lied and stopped her from going to the Hall to see Sir Charles.

"That night Stapleton took his dog to a hiding place near the gate. When he saw Sir Charles he let the hound loose. It jumped over the gate and chased the poor baronet who died of fear. The idea was so clever because the real murderer could not be proved guilty. His only help came from an animal who couldn't talk.

"Dr. Mortimer told Stapleton about the heir coming from Canada. Stapleton's first idea was to possibly kill Sir Henry in London before he ever came to Devonshire. He brought his wife with him to London because he didn't trust her alone. She was the one who sent the letter of warning to the new baronet.

"It was very important for Stapleton to get some piece of clothing belonging to Sir Henry so that he could later use it for the dog. He went to the hotel. There he paid money to a servant who helped him.

15. Looking Back

The first shoe was new and had no smell, so he had to get a second one.

"The next morning our friends came to visit, followed always by Stapleton in his cab. That's when he realized that I was taking the case. He decided to return to Dartmoor and wait for the baronet."

"One moment," I said. "What happened to the hound when its master was in London?"

"For many years the Stapletons had an old servant named Anthony. He recently disappeared and escaped from England. He is the one who took care of the dog when the master was away.

"You may remember that I closely examined the newspaper letter. It's because I could smell a lady's perfume. That's when I began to suspect the Stapletons.

"It was my plan to watch Stapleton. I knew, however, that I had to be alone to do that. So it was necessary to trick everyone, including you, Watson. I told everyone I was busy in London and came there secretly. Actually, I only spent a few nights on the moor in that stone hut. I was in Coombe Tracey most of the time, and Cartwright was there to help me.

"In one of your reports, Watson, you told me about Stapleton's days as a schoolmaster. I then knew exactly who they were. However, I needed to catch Stapleton in the act of murder in order to prove the case in court. That's why I had to use Sir Henry, alone and unprotected. I am truly sorry for the shock to his nerves. He will be fine again soon. I also hope his feelings recover from being tricked by Mrs. Stapleton.

"I believe that Stapleton controlled his wife with both love and fear. She really didn't want anyone to be hurt. She tried to warn Sir Henry while also protecting her husband. The night that Sir Henry came to dinner she tried to stop her husband. They had a terrible fight. He told her about another woman, and she hated him. He tied her up so that he could carry out his murder. He hoped that later she would forgive him. But she never would.

"Watson, without my notes I can't give you many more details."

"There is just one more question. If Stapleton had become the heir to Baskerville Hall how could he suddenly tell people who he really was after all this time?"

"With great difficulty. I really don't have the answer, but I believe there were three choices. He might return to South America and claim the property from there through the British government; or he might try to change his appearance and name completely; or, he might pay a companion to take his place at Baskerville Hall while he kept most of the money. I'm sure this cruel and clever man would have found some way to do it. And now, my dear Watson, perhaps we should go out and have a nice dinner."

Word List

- LEVEL 1、2は本文で使われている全ての語を掲載しています。
  LEVEL 3以上は、中学校レベルの語を含みません。ただし、本文で特殊な意味で使われている場合、その意味のみを掲載しています。
- 語形が規則変化する語の見出しは原形で示しています。不規則変化語は本文中で使われている形になっています。
- 一般的な意味を紹介していますので、一部の語で本文で実際に使われている品詞や意味と合っていないことがあります。
- 品詞は以下のように示しています。

名 名詞	代 代名詞	形 形容詞	副 副詞	動 動詞	助動 助動詞
前 前置詞	接 接続詞	間 間投詞	冠 冠詞	略 略語	俗 俗語
熟 熟語	頭 接頭語	尾 接尾語	記 記号	関 関係代名詞	

A

- **accident** 名 ①(不慮の)事故, 災難 ②偶然
- **account** 名 説明, 報告
- **act** 名 行為, 行い 動 ①行動する ②機能する ③演じる
- **actually** 副 実際に, 本当に, 実は
- **address** 名 ①住所, アドレス ②演説 動 ①あて名を書く ②演説をする, 話しかける
- **Admiral** 名 海軍提督, 艦隊司令官 Admiral Baskerville バスカヴィル海軍少将
- **admit** 動 認める, 許可する, 入れる
- **adventure** 名 冒険 動 危険をおかす
- **advice** 名 忠告, 助言, 意見
- **affair** 名 ①事柄, 事件 ②《-s》業務, 仕事, やるべきこと
- **affect** 動 ①影響する ②(病気などが)おかす ③ふりをする 名 感情, 欲望
- **afraid** 熟 《be》afraid of 〜を恐れる, 〜を怖がる
- **Africa** 名 アフリカ《大陸》
- **after** 動 〜の後を追って, 〜を捜して 熟 hill after hill 小山に次ぐ小山
- **ah** 間 《驚き・悲しみ・賞賛などを表して》ああ, やっぱり
- **ahead** 副 先んじて
- **all** 熟 first of all まず第一に
- **allow** 動 ①許す, 《−…to 〜》…が〜するのを可能にする, …に〜させておく ②与える
- **although** 接 〜だけれども, 〜にもかかわらず, たとえ〜でも
- **America** 名 アメリカ《国名・大陸》
- **American** 形 アメリカ(人)の 名 アメリカ人
- **amount** 名 ①量, 額 ②《the−》合計 動 (総計〜に)なる
- **ancient** 形 昔の, 古代の
- **anger** 名 怒り white with anger 怒りで顔色が白くなる
- **animal-like** 形 動物のような
- **another** 熟 one another お互い
- **Anthony** 名 アンソニー《人名》
- **anxious** 形 ①心配な, 不安な ②切望して 《be》anxious for 〜を切望している
- **anymore** 副 《通例否定文, 疑問文で》今はもう, これ以上, これから

128

Word List

- **anyone** 代 ①《疑問文・条件節で》誰か ②《否定文で》誰も（〜ない）③《肯定文で》誰でも
- **anyway** 副 ①いずれにせよ、ともかく ②どんな方法でも
- **anywhere** 副 どこかへ[に]、どこにも、どこへも、どこにでも
- **apart** 副 ①ばらばらに、離れて ②別にして、それだけで
- **appear** 動 ①現れる、見えてくる ②（〜のように）見える、〜らしい
- **appearance** 名 ①現れること、出現 ②外見、印象
- **appointment** 名 ①（会合などの）約束、予約 ②任命、指名
- **approach** 動 ①接近する ②話を持ちかける 名 接近、(〜へ) 近づく道
- **armchair** 名 ひじ掛けいす、ひじ置き
- **around** 熟 look around for 〜を捜し求める
- **arrange** 動 ①並べる、整える ②取り決める ③準備する、手はずを整える
- **article** 名 ①（法令・誓約などの）箇条、項目 ②（新聞・雑誌などの）記事、論文
- **artist** 名 芸術家
- **as** 熟 as if あたかも〜のように as of now 今のところ as to 〜に関しては
- **ash** 名 ①灰、燃えかす ②《-es》遺骨、なきがら
- **asleep** 形 ①眠って（いる状態の）②（手足が）しびれている 副 ①眠って、休止して ②（手足が）しびれて fall asleep 眠り込む、寝入る
- **assume** 動 ①仮定する、当然のことと思う ②引き受ける
- **assure** 動 ①保障する、請け負う ②確信をもって言う
- **attach** 動 ①取り付ける、添える ②付随する、帰属する
- **attack** 動 ①襲う、攻める ②非難する（病気が）おかす 名 ①攻撃、非難 ②発作、発病 heart attack 心臓麻痺
- **author** 名 著者、作家 動 著作する、創作する
- **avenue** 名 ①並木道 ②《A-, Ave.》〜通り、〜街
- **average** 名 平均（値）、並み on (the) average 平均して 形 平均の、普通の 動 平均して〜になる
- **avoid** 動 避ける、(〜を) しないようにする
- **awake** 動 ①目覚めさせる ②目覚める 形 目が覚めて
- **away** 熟 get away 逃げる run away 走り去る、逃げ出す
- **awful** 形 ①ひどい、不愉快な ②恐ろしい 副 ひどく、とても

B

- **back** 熟 lean back 後ろにもたれる
- **badly** 副 ①悪く、まずく、へたに ②とても、ひどく
- **Baker Street** ベーカー街《地名》
- **band** 名 ①ひも、帯 ②楽団 ③縞模様 動 ①ひもで縛る ②団結する[させる]
- **barely** 副 ①かろうじて、やっと ②ほぼ、もう少しで
- **baronet** 名 準男爵
- **Barrymore** 名 バリモア《人名》
- **Baskerville** 名 バスカヴィル《人名》 Baskerville Hall バスカヴィル邸
- **battle** 名 戦闘、戦い 動 戦う
- **be** 熟 can be of any help to 〜の役に立つことができる
- **beard** 名 あごひげ
- **bearded** 形 あごひげを生やした

- **beast** 名 ①動物, けもの ②けもののような人, 非常にいやな人[物]
- **beaten** 動 beat（打つ）の過去分詞 形 打たれた, 打ち負かされた, 疲れ切った
- **beauty** 名 ①美, 美しい人[物] ②《the -》美点
- **bedroom** 名 寝室
- **begin** 熟 to begin with はじめに We end where we began. 我々は振り出しのところでおしまいだ。
- **behind** 前 ①〜の後ろに, 〜の背後に ②〜に遅れて, 〜に劣って 副 ①後ろに, 背後に ②遅れて, 劣って leave behind 置いて来る
- **bell** 名 ベル, 鈴, 鐘 動 ①（ベル・鐘が）鳴る ②ベル[鈴]をつける
- **belong to** 〜に属する
- **below** 前 ①〜より下に ②〜以下の, 〜より劣る 副 下に[へ]
- **beneath** 前 〜の下に[の], 〜より低い 副 下に, 劣って
- **bent** 動 bend（曲がる）の過去, 過去分詞 形 ①曲がった ②熱中した, 決心した 名（生まれつきの）好み, 傾向
- **Beryl** 名 ベリル《人名》Beryl Garcia ベリル・ガルシア Beryl Stapleton ベリル・ステイプルトン
- **beside** 前 ①〜のそばに, 〜と並んで ②〜と比べると ③〜とはずれて
- **besides** 前 ①〜に加えて, 〜のほかに ②《否定文・疑問文で》〜を除いて 副 その上, さらに
- **bet** 動 賭ける 名 賭け, 掛け金（の対象）
- **beyond** 前 〜を越えて, 〜の向こうに 副 向こうに
- **bit** 動 bite（かむ）の過去, 過去分詞 名 ①小片, 少量 ②《a -》少し, ちょっと ③（情報量単位の）ビット
- **bite** 動 かむ, かじる 名 かむこと, かみ傷, ひと口
- **black oak** クロガシ
- **black-bearded** 形 黒いあごひげを生やした
- **blackness** 名 暗さ, 暗黒
- **blame** 動 とがめる, 非難する 名 ①責任, 罪 ②非難
- **blanket** 名 毛布 動 毛布でくるむ
- **bless** 動 神の加護を祈る, 〜を祝福する God bless you! 神のご加護がありますように。
- **blew** 動 blow（吹く）の過去
- **blindly** 副 盲目的に, むやみに
- **blood** 名 ①血, 血液 ②血統, 家柄 ③気質
- **bloody** 形 血だらけの, 血なまぐさい, むごい 副 ひどく
- **blow** 動 ①（風が）吹く,（風が）〜を吹き飛ばす ②息を吹く,（鼻を）かむ ③破裂する ④吹奏する 名 ①（風の）ひと吹き, 突風 ②（楽器の）吹奏 ③打撃
- **bone** 名 ①骨,《-s》骨格 ②《-s》要点, 骨組み 動（魚・肉）の骨をとる
- **bookcase** 名 本箱
- **bore** 動 bear（耐える）の過去 ②退屈させる ③穴があく, 穴をあける 名 退屈な人[もの], うんざりすること
- **bottom** 名 ①底, 下部, すそ野, ふもと, 最下位, 根底 ②尻 形 底の, 根底の
- **bottomless** 形 ①底なしの, 底抜けの ②際限のない, とても深い ③計り知れない, 不可解な
- **Bradley** 名 ブラッドリー《タバコ会社の名前, または商標》
- **brain** 名 ①脳 ②知力
- **brave** 形 勇敢な 動 勇敢に立ち向かう
- **bravery** 名 勇敢さ, 勇気ある行動
- **breakdown** 熟 nervous breakdown 神経衰弱, ノイローゼ
- **breathe** 動 ①呼吸する ②ひと息つく, 休息する

Word List

- **briefly** 副 短く, 簡潔に
- **brighten** 動 輝かせる, 快活にさせる
- **brightly** 副 明るく, 輝いて, 快活に
- **bring up** 連れて行く
- **British** 形 ①英国人の ②イギリス英語の 名 英国人
- **broad** 形 ①幅の広い ②寛大な ③明白な 副 すっかり, 十分に
- **builder** 名 建設者
- **burst** 動 ①爆発する[させる] ②破裂する[させる] burst into ～ ～に飛び込む, 急に～する
- **bush** 名 低木, やぶ, 未開墾地
- **butler** 名 執事
- **by** 熟 by God 神かけて, 本当に by Heaven 神にかけて By whom? 誰に?

C

- **C.C.H.** 略 Charing Cross Hospital チャリング・クロス病院
- **cab** 名 タクシー
- **call in** ～を呼ぶ
- **calmly** 副 落ち着いて, 静かに
- **can be of any help to** ～の役に立つことができる
- **Canada** 名 カナダ《国名》
- **candle** 名 ろうそく
- **carriage** 名 ①馬車 ②乗り物, 車
- **carry** 熟 carry off さらって行く carry on 続ける carry out [計画を]実行する
- **Cartwright** 名 カートライト《人名》
- **case** 熟 have a case 告訴する
- **caught** 熟 get caught 逮捕される
- **Celtic** 形 ケルト(人)の
- **central** 形 中央の, 主要な
- **certain** 形 ①確実な, 必ず～する ②(人が)確信した ③ある ④いくらかの 代 (～の中の)いくつか
- **certainly** 副 ①確かに, 必ず ②《返答に用いて》もちろん, そのとおり, 承知しました
- **chance** 熟 take a chance 一か八かやってみる
- **chapter** 名 (書物の)章
- **character** 名 ①特性, 個性 ②(小説・劇などの)登場人物 ③文字, 記号 ④品性, 人格
- **charge** 動 ①(代金を)請求する ②(～を…に)負わせる ③命じる 名 ①請求金額, 料金 ②責任 ③非難, 告発 in charge of ～ ～を担当して, ～の責任を負って
- **Charing Cross** チャリング・クロス《地名》
- **Charles Baskerville** チャールズ・バスカヴィル《人名》
- **chase** 動 ①追跡する, 追い[探し]求める ②追い立てる
- **check** 動 ①照合する, 検査する ②阻止[妨害]する ③(所持品を)預ける 名 ①照合, 検査 ②小切手 ③(突然の)停止, 阻止(するもの) ④伝票, 勘定書
- **cheerful** 形 上機嫌の, 元気のよい, (人を)気持ちよくさせる
- **chest** 名 ①大きな箱, 戸棚, たんす ②金庫 ③胸, 肺
- **chief** 名 頭, 長, 親分 形 最高位の, 第一の, 主要な
- **choice** 名 選択(の範囲・自由), えり好み, 選ばれた人[物] 形 精選した
- **churchman** 名 牧師
- **cigar** 名 葉巻
- **cigarette** 名 (紙巻)たばこ
- **circle** stone circle 環状列石
- **circumstance** 名 ①(周囲の)事情, 状況, 環境 ②《-s》(人の)境遇, 生活状態

THE HOUND OF THE BASKERVILLES

- **claim** 動①主張する ②要求する, 請求する 名①主張, 断言 ②要求, 請求
- **Clayton** 名 John Clayton ジョン・クレイトン《人名》
- **clean-faced** 形 きれいにひげを剃った
- **clear** 形①はっきりした, 明白な ②澄んだ ③(よく)晴れた 動①はっきりさせる ②片づける ③晴れる 副①はっきりと ②すっかり, 完全に
- **clearly** 副①明らかに, はっきりと ②《返答に用いて》そのとおり
- **clever** 形①頭のよい, 利口な ②器用な, 上手な
- **climb over** 〜を乗り越える
- **closely** 副①密接に ②念入りに, 詳しく ③ぴったりと
- **clothe** 動服を着せる, 《受け身形で》(〜を)着ている, (〜の)格好をする
- **clue** 名手がかり, 糸口
- **coast** 名海岸, 沿岸 動①滑降する ②(〜の)沿岸を航行する ③楽々とやり遂げる
- **cold-blooded** 形冷血な
- **coldly** 副冷たく, よそよそしく
- **collection** 名収集, 収蔵物
- **come** 熟 come down 田舎へ来る come in 〜 from 〜から来る come out friends 友人になる come out 現れる
- **comfort** 名①快適さ, 満足 ②慰め ③安楽 動心地よくする, ほっとさせる, 慰める
- **comfortable** 形快適な, 心地いい
- **Commons** 熟 House of Commons 庶民院, 下院
- **companion** 名①友, 仲間, 連れ ②添えもの, つきもの
- **compare** 動①比較する, 対照する ②たとえる (as) compared with [to] 〜と比較して, 〜に比べれば
- **complete** 形完全な, まったくの, 完成した 動完成させる
- **completely** 副完全に, すっかり
- **concern** 動①関係する, 《be -ed in [with] 〜》〜に関係している ②心配させる, 《be -ed about [for] 〜》〜を心配する 名①関心事 ②関心, 心配 ③関係, 重要性
- **condition** 名①(健康)状態, 境遇 ②《-s》状況, 様子 ③条件 動適応させる, 条件づける on the condition that もし〜なら
- **contain** 動①含む, 入っている ②(感情などを)抑える
- **continuous** 形連続的な, 継続する, 絶え間ない
- **control** 動①管理[支配]する ②抑制する, コントロールする 名①管理, 支配(力) ②抑制 have control over 〜を支配[コントロール]する in control 〜を支配して, 〜を掌握している
- **convenient** 形便利な, 好都合な
- **convict** 動有罪を宣告する 名罪人, 囚人
- **Coombe Tracey** クーム・トレーシー《地名》
- **copy** 名①コピー, 写し ②(書籍の)一部, 冊 ③広告文 動写す, まねる, コピーする
- **correct** 形正しい, 適切な, りっぱな 動(誤りを)訂正する, 直す
- **Costa Rican** 形コスタリカ(人)の
- **cotton** 名①綿, 綿花 ②綿織物, 綿糸
- **countryside** 名地方, 田舎
- **county** 名郡, 州
- **couple** 名①2つ, 対 ②夫婦, 一組 ③数個 動つなぐ, つながる, 関連させる

WORD LIST

- **court** 名①中庭, コート ②法廷, 裁判所 ③宮廷, 宮殿
- **cover** 動①覆う, 包む, 隠す ②扱う, (〜に)わたる, 及ぶ ③代わりを務める ④補う 名覆い, カバー
- **cow** 名雌牛, 乳牛
- **co-worker** 名同僚, 仕事仲間
- **crazily** 副気の狂ったように
- **crazy** 形①狂気の, ばかげた, 無茶な ②夢中の, 熱狂的な
- **create** 動創造する, 生み出す, 引き起こす
- **creature** 名(神の)創造物, 生物, 動物
- **crime** 名①(法律上の)罪, 犯罪 ②悪事, よくない行為
- **criminal** 形犯罪の, 罪深い, 恥ずべき 名犯罪者, 犯人
- **cruel** 形残酷な, 厳しい
- **crush** 動押しつぶす, 砕く, 粉々にする 名押しつぶすこと
- **cry over** 〜を嘆く
- **curious** 形好奇心の強い, 珍しい, 奇妙な, 知りたがる
- **curl** 名巻き毛, 渦巻状のもの 動カールする, 巻きつく
- **curly** 形巻き毛の
- **curly-haired** 形縮れ毛の
- **curse** 動のろう, ののしる 名のろい(の言葉), 悪態
- **curve** 名曲線, カーブ 動曲がる, 曲げる
- **cut out** 切り取る, 切り抜く
- **cut-out** 名切り抜き

D

- **dark-black** 形真っ黒な
- **darkness** 名暗さ, 暗やみ
- **Dartmoor** 名ダートムア《地名》
- **date** 動年代を定める
- **daytime** 名昼間
- **dead** 形 **fall dead** 倒れて死ぬ **in the dead of night** 真夜中に
- **deadly** 形命にかかわる, 痛烈な, 破壊的な 副ひどく, 極度に
- **deal** 動①分配する ②《 – with [in] 〜》〜を扱う 名①取引, 扱い ②(不特定の)量, 額 **a good [great] deal (of 〜)** かなり[ずいぶん・大量](の〜), 多数(の〜)
- **death** 名①死, 死ぬこと ②《the – 》終えん, 消滅
- **decision** 名①決心 ②決定, 判決 ③決断(力)
- **deeply** 副深く, 非常に
- **defend** 動防ぐ, 守る, 弁護する
- **delay** 動遅らせる, 延期する 名遅延, 延期, 猶予
- **delight** 動喜ぶ, 喜ばす, 楽しむ, 楽しませる 名喜び, 愉快
- **deliver** 動①配達する, 伝える ②達成する, 果たす
- **demand** 動①要求する, 尋ねる ②必要とする 名①要求, 請求 ②需要
- **deny** 動否定する, 断る, 受けつけない
- **depart** 動①出発する ②(常道などから)はずれる
- **depend** 動《 – on [upon] 〜》①〜を頼る, 〜をあてにする ②〜による
- **describe** 動(言葉で)描写する, 特色を述べる, 説明する
- **deserve** 動(〜を)受けるに足る, 値する, (〜して)当然である
- **designer** 名デザイナー, 設計者
- **desire** 動強く望む, 欲する 名欲望, 欲求, 願望
- **Desmond** 名デズモンド《人名》
- **despair** 動絶望する, あきらめる 名絶望, 自暴自棄

133

- **destroy** 動 破壊する, 絶滅させる, 無効にする
- **detail** 名 ①細部,《-s》詳細 ②《-s》個人情報 動 詳しく述べる
- **detective** 名 探偵, 刑事 形 探偵の
- **develop** 動 ①発達する[させる] ②開発する
- **development** 名 ①発達, 発展 ②開発
- **devilish** 形 ①悪魔のような ②のろわしい, 極悪な
- **Devon** 名 デボンシャー (Devonshire)《地名》
- **Devonshire** 名 デボンシャー《地名》
- **diary** 名 日記
- **die of** 〜がもとで死ぬ
- **difficulty** 名 ①むずかしさ ②難局, 支障, 苦情, 異議 ③《-ties》財政困難
- **dig** 動 ①掘る ②小突く ③探る 名 ①突き ②掘ること, 発掘
- **dine** 動 食事をする, ごちそうする
- **dining room** 食事室, 食堂
- **direct** 形 まっすぐな, 直接の, 率直な, 露骨な 副 まっすぐに, 直接に 動 ①指導する, 監督する ②(目・注意・努力などを)向ける
- **directly** 副 ①じかに ②まっすぐに ③ちょうど
- **directory** 名 ①住所氏名録, 建物案内板 ②訓令集, 規則書 Medical Directory 医師録
- **dirty** 形 ①汚い, 汚れた ②卑劣な, 不正な 動 汚す
- **disappear** 動 見えなくなる, 姿を消す, なくなる
- **disappoint** 動 失望させる, がっかりさせる
- **disappointment** 名 失望
- **disease** 名 病気, 不健全な状態
- **dishonored** 形 名誉を汚された
- **distance** 名 距離, 隔たり, 遠方 at a distance 少し離れて
- **distant** 形 ①遠い, 隔たった ②よそよそしい, 距離のある
- **divorce** 動 離婚する 名 離婚, 分離
- **doorbell** 名 玄関の呼び鈴[ベル]
- **doorman** (ホテルの)ドアマン
- **door-step** 名 戸口の踏み段[上がり段]
- **dot** 名 ①点, 小数点 ②水玉(模様)
- **double** 形 ①2倍の, 二重の ②対の 副 ①2倍に ②対で 動 ①2倍になる[する] ②兼ねる
- **doubt** 名 疑い, 不確かなこと 動 疑う
- **down** 熟 come down 田舎へ来る put down 下に置く, 下ろす throw down 投げ出す, 放棄する
- **downstairs** 副 階下で, 下の部屋で 形 階下の 名 階下
- **Dr.** 名 〜博士,《医者に対して》〜先生
- **draw** 動 ①引く, 引っ張る ②描く ③引き分けになる[する]
- **driver** 名 ①運転手 ②(馬車の)御者
- **drop off** 〜から(取れて)落ちる
- **drove** 動 drive (車で行く)の過去
- **drunk** 熟 get drunk 酔う, 酩酊する
- **drunken** 形 酔っ払った
- **dry-land** 名 乾燥地 dry-land marker stick 乾燥地の目印棒
- **dug** dig (掘る)の過去, 過去分詞
- **dull** 形 ①退屈な, 鈍い, くすんだ, ぼんやりした 動 鈍くする[する]
- **duty** 名 ①義務(感), 責任 ②職務, 任務, 関税

E

- **eager** 形 ①熱心な ②《be-for 〜》

Word List

~を切望している，《be - to ~》しきりに~したがっている
- **eagerly** 副 熱心に，しきりに
- **eagerness** 名 熱心，熱望
- **earth** How on earth ~ 一体どうやったら
- **easily** 副 ①容易に，たやすく，苦もなく ②気楽に
- **edge** 名 ①刃 ②端，縁 動 ①刃をつける，鋭くする ②縁どる，縁に沿って進む
- **educate** 動 教育する，(~するように)訓練する
- **effort** 名 努力(の成果)
- **electric** 形 電気の，電動の
- **emotion** 名 感激，感動，感情
- **emotional** 形 ①感情の，心理的な ②感情的な，感激しやすい
- **end** 熟 We end where we began. 我々は振り出しのところでおしまいだ。
- **enemy** 名 敵
- **England** 名 ①イングランド ②英国
- **enjoyment** 名 楽しむこと，喜び
- **entire** 形 全体の，完全な，まったくの
- **error** 名 誤り，間違い，過失
- **escape** 動 逃げる，免れる，もれる 名 逃亡，脱出，もれ
- **ever since** その後ずっと
- **everyone** 代 誰でも，皆
- **everything** 代 すべてのこと[もの]，何でも，何もかも
- **evidence** 名 ①証拠，証人 ②形跡
- **evil** 形 ①邪悪な ②有害な，不吉な 名 ①邪悪 ②害，わざわい，不幸 副 悪く
- **evil-looking** 形 不気味な
- **exact** 形 正確な，厳密な，きちょうめんな
- **examine** 動 試験する，調査[検査]する，診察する
- **excellent** 形 優れた，優秀な
- **except** 前 ~を除いて，~のほかは except for ~ ~を除いて，~がなければ 接 ~ということを除いて
- **excitement** 名 興奮(すること)
- **excuse oneself** 辞退する
- **expect** 動 予期[予測]する，(当然のこととして)期待する
- **expense** 名 ①出費，費用 ②犠牲，代価 at any expense どんなに費用がかかっても，どんな犠牲を払っても at the expense of ~ ~を犠牲にして
- **extra** 形 余分の，臨時の 名 ①余分なもの ②エキストラ 副 余分に
- **eyeglasses** 名 メガネ

F

- **fail** 動 ①失敗する，落第する[させる] ②《-to ~》~し損なう，~できない ③失望させる never [not] fail to ~ 必ず~する 名 失敗，落第点
- **faint** 形 かすかな，弱い，ぼんやりした 動 気絶する 名 気絶，失神
- **fair** 形 ①正しい，公平[正当]な ②快晴の ③色白の，金髪の ④かなりの ⑤《古》美しい 副 ①公平に，きれいに ②見事に
- **faithful** 形 忠実な，正確な
- **fall dead** 倒れて死ぬ
- **fallen** 動 fall (落ちる)の過去分詞 形 落ちた，倒れた
- **false** 形 うその，間違った，にせの，不誠実な 副 不誠実に
- **falsely** 副 不当に
- **far off** ずっと遠くに，はるかかなたに
- **farmer** 名 農民，農場経営者

The Hound of the Baskervilles

- **farmhouse** 名 農場内の家屋, 農家
- **farmland** 名 農地
- **fate** 名 《時に F-》運命, 宿命 ②破滅, 悲運 動 (〜の) 運命にある
- **fault** 名 ①欠点, 短所 ②過失, 誤り **at fault** 誤って, 非難されるべき **find fault with** 〜 〜のあら探しをする 動 とがめる
- **fear** 名 ①恐れ ②心配, 不安 動 ①恐れる ②心配する
- **fearful** 形 ①恐ろしい ②心配な, 気づかって
- **feather** 名 羽, 《-s》羽毛
- **feature** 名 ①特徴, 特色 ②顔の一部, 《-s》目立ち ③(ラジオ・テレビ・新聞などの)特集 動 ①(〜の)特徴になる ②呼び物にする
- **feet** 熟 **on one's feet** 立っている状態で, 自分の足で
- **fellow** 名 ①仲間, 同僚 ②人, やつ 形 仲間の, 同士の
- **Fernworthy** 名 ファーンワージー《地名》
- **fever** 名 ①熱, 熱狂 ②熱病 動 発熱させる, 熱狂させる
- **fiery** 形 ①火の, 燃えさかる ②火のように赤い
- **figure** 名 ①人[物]の姿, 形 ②図(形) ③数字 動 ①描写する, 想像する ②計算する ③目立つ, (〜として)現れる **figure out** (問題などを)解く, 理解する
- **final** 形 最後の, 決定的な 名 ①最後のもの ②期末[最終]試験 ③《-s》決勝戦
- **fireplace** 名 暖炉
- **firm** 形 堅い, しっかりした, 断固とした 副 しっかりと
- **first of all** まず第一に
- **first-class** 形 ①一流の, (乗り物の)一等の ②(郵便で)第一種の 副 一等で, 第一種郵便で

- **fit** 形 ①適当な, 相応な ②体の調子がよい 動 合致[適合]する, 合致させる 名 発作, けいれん, 一時的興奮
- **fix** 動 ①固定する[させる] ②修理する ③決定する ④用意する, 整える
- **flame** 名 炎, (炎のような)輝き 動 燃え上がる, (顔などが)さっと赤らむ
- **flash** 名 閃光, きらめき 動 ①閃光を発する ②さっと動く, ひらめく **flash back** (記憶などが)突然戻る
- **flow** 動 流れ出る, 流れる, あふれる 名 ①流出 ②流ちょう(なこと)
- **fog** 名 ①濃霧, 煙 ②混乱, 当惑 動 曇らせる, 当惑させる
- **foggy** 形 霧の多い, 霧の立ちこめた
- **fold** 名 折り目, ひだ 動 ①折りたたむ, 包む ②(手を)組む
- **fool** 名 ①ばか者, おろかな人 ②道化師 **make a fool of** 〜 〜をばかにする 動 ばかにする, だます, ふざける
- **foolish** 形 おろかな, ばかばかしい
- **foolishly** 副 おろかに
- **footprint** 名 足型, 足跡
- **footstep** 名 足音, 歩み
- **for** 熟 **for now** 今のところ, ひとまず **pass for** 〜で通る **reach for** 〜に手を伸ばす, 〜を取ろうとする **send for** 〜を呼びにやる, 〜を呼び寄せる
- **force** 名 力, 勢い 動 ①強制する, 力ずくで〜する, 余儀なく〜させる ②押しやる, 押し込む
- **forceful** 形 力強い, 説得力のある
- **forgetful** 形 忘れっぽい, 無頓着な
- **forgive** 動 許す, 免除する
- **forgiven** 動 forgive (許す) の過去分詞
- **form** 名 ①形, 形式 ②書式 **take form** (物事が)形をとる, 具体化する 動 形づくる
- **former** ①前の, 先の, 以前の

②《the –》(二者のうち)前者の

- **forth** 副 前へ, 外へ　and so forth [on] など, その他
- **fortune** 名 ①富, 財産　②幸運, 繁栄, チャンス　③運命, 運勢
- **forward** 形 ①前方の, 前方へ向かう　②将来の　③先の　副 ①前方に　②将来に向けて　③先へ, 進んで　look forward to ～[～ ing] ～を期待する　動 ①転送する　②進める　名 前衛
- **Foulmire** 名 ファウルマイア《農家》
- **Frankland** 名 フランクランド《人名》
- **friend** 熟 come out friends 友人になる
- **friendly** 形 親しみのある, 親切な, 友情のこもった　副 友好的に, 親切に
- **friendship** 名 友人であること, 友情
- **frighten** 動 驚かせる, びっくりさせる
- **front desk** [ホテルの]フロント
- **full** 形 完全な, 不足していない　熟 full day 丸一日
- **fully** 副 十分に, 完全に, まるまる
- **further** 形 いっそう遠い, その上の, なおいっそうの　副 いっそう遠く, その上に, もっと　動 促進する

G

- **gain** 動 ①得る, 増す　②進歩する, 進む　名 ①増加, 進歩　②利益, 得ること, 獲得
- **Garcia** 名 Beryl Garcia ベリル・ガルシア《人名》
- **gardenhouse** 名 庭園にある小さな建物
- **general** 形 ①全体の, 一般の, 普通の　②おおよその　③(職位の)高い, 上級の　in general 一般に, たいてい　名 大将, 将軍
- **generous** 形 ①寛大な, 気前のよい　②豊富な
- **gentle** 形 ①優しい, 温和な　②柔らかな
- **German** 形 ドイツ(人・語)の　名 ①ドイツ人　②ドイツ語
- **get** 熟 get away 逃げる　get caught 逮捕される　get drunk う, 酩酊する　get into trouble with ～とトラブルを起こす　get on 乗る　get to 到着する, 到達する　get used to ～に慣れる
- **giant** 名 ①巨人, 大男　②巨匠　形 巨大な, 偉大な
- **gift** 名 ①贈り物　②(天賦の)才能　動 授ける
- **give** 熟 I give you my word. 約束するよ。保証するよ。
- **glance** 名 ①ちらっと見ること, 一べつ　②ひらめき　③かすめること　動 ①ちらりと見る　②かすめる
- **glory** 名 栄光, 名誉, 繁栄
- **glow** 動 ①(火が)白熱して輝く　②(体が)ほてる　名 ①白熱, 輝き　②ほてり, 熱情
- **go** 熟 go for ～に襲いかかる　there goes [チャンスなどが] 行ってしまう
- **God** 熟 by God 神かけて, 本当に　God bless you! 神のご加護がありますように。　My God. おや, まあ　Thank God. ありがたい
- **godless** 形 神を否定した, 神を恐れぬ
- **golden** 形 ①金色の　②金製の　③貴重な
- **good** 熟 Good day. ご機嫌よう。　Good Heavens. 困った, まあ, とんでもない
- **good-bye** 間 さようなら　名 別れのあいさつ
- **good-looking** 形 顔立ちのよい, ハンサムな, きれいな

THE HOUND OF THE BASKERVILLES

- **government** 名 政治, 政府, 支配
- **gradually** 副 だんだんと
- **grass** 名 草, 牧草(地), 芝生 動 草[芝生]で覆う[覆われる]
- **grassy** 形 草で覆われた, 草のような
- **grateful** 形 感謝する, ありがたく思う
- **grave** 名 墓 形 重要な, 厳粛な, 落ち着いた
- **greatly** 副 大いに
- **greet** 動 ①あいさつする ②(喜んで)迎える
- **Grimpen** 名 グリンペン《地名》 Grimpen Mire グリンペン大沼 Grimpen Road グリンペン街道
- **guard** 名 ①警戒, 見張り ②番人 動 番をする, 監視する, 守る
- **guess at** ～を推測する
- **guest** 名 客, ゲスト
- **guiding stick** 目印の棒
- **guilty** 形 有罪の, やましい
- **gun** 名 銃, 大砲 動 銃で撃つ

H

- **ha** 間 ほう, まあ, おや《驚き・悲しみ・不満・喜び・笑い声などを表す》
- **had** 熟 I wish I had been there. 自分がそこにいられればよかったのに。
- **half-pound** 半ポンド
- **halfway** 副 中間[中途]で, 不完全に 形 中間[中途]の, 不完全な
- **hall** 名 公会堂, ホール, 大広間, 玄関 Baskerville Hall バスカヴィル邸 Lafter Hall ラフター邸
- **hallway** 名 玄関, 廊下
- **hand** 熟 put up one's hand 手を挙げる
- **handle** 名 取っ手, 握り 動 ①手を触れる ②操縦する, 取り扱う
- **handsome** 形 端正な(顔立ちの), りっぱな, (男性が)ハンサムな
- **handwriting** 名 ①手書き, 肉筆 ②筆跡, 書体
- **hang** 動 かかる, かける, つるす, ぶら下がる hang on しがみつく, がんばる, (電話を)切らずに待つ hang up つるす, 電話を切る 名 ①かかり具合 ②《the-》扱い方, こつ
- **happily** 副 幸福に, 楽しく, うまく, 幸いにも
- **hardly** 副 ①ほとんど～でない, わずかに ②厳しく, かろうじて
- **hard-working** 形 よく働く
- **harm** 名 害, 損害, 危害 動 傷つける, 損なう
- **hate** 動 嫌う, 憎む, (～するのを)いやがる 名 憎しみ
- **hateful** 形 憎らしい, 忌まわしい
- **have** 熟 have a case 告訴する have control over ～を支配[コントロール]する
- **healthy** 形 健康な, 健全な, 健康によい
- **hear of** ～について聞く
- **heart attack** 心臓麻痺
- **heaven** 名 ①天国 ②天国のようなところ[状態], 楽園 ③空 ④《H-》神 by Heaven 神にかけて Good Heavens. 困った, まあ, とんでもない
- **height** 名 ①高さ, 身長 ②《the-》絶頂, 真っ盛り ③高台, 丘
- **heir** 名 相続人, 後継者
- **hell** 名 地獄, 地獄のようなところ[状態]
- **hell-hound** 名 地獄の番犬
- **help** 熟 can be of any help to ～の役に立つことができる
- **Henry Baskerville** ヘンリー・バスカヴィル《人名》

WORD LIST

- **hide** 動隠れる, 隠す, 隠れて見えない, 秘密にする
- **High Barrow** ハイ・バロー《地名》
- **hill** 熟 hill after hill 小山に次ぐ小山
- **hillside** 名丘の中腹［斜面］
- **hilltop** 名丘の頂上
- **hitting sound** ぶつかる音
- **hmmm** 間ふうむ, なるほど
- **hobby** 名趣味, 得意なこと
- **Holmes** 名 Sherlock Holmes シャーロック・ホームズ《人名》
- **honest** 形①正直な, 誠実な, 心からの ②公正な, 感心な
- **honestly** 副正直に
- **honesty** 名正直, 誠実
- **honor** 名①名誉, 光栄, 信用 ②節操, 自尊心 in honor of ～ ～に敬意を表して, ～を記念して 動尊敬する, 栄誉を与える
- **honorable** 形①尊敬すべき, 立派な ②名誉ある ③高貴な
- **hop** 動①(片足で)ぴょんと飛ぶ, 飛び越える, 飛び乗る ②飛行機で行く, 短い旅行をする 名①ぴょんと飛ぶこと, 跳躍 ②ホップ《クワ科多年生の草の総称》
- **hound** 名猟犬
- **hour** 熟 in one hour 1時間で, 1時間以内に
- **House of Commons** 庶民院, 下院
- **house-doctor** 名住込み医師
- **housekeeper** 名家政婦
- **How on earth** ～ 一体どうやったら
- **however** 副たとえ～でも 接けれども, だが
- **huge** 形巨大な, ばく大な
- **Hugo Baskerville** ヒューゴ・バスカヴィル《人名》
- **humble** 形つつましい, 粗末な 動卑しめる, 謙虚にさせる
- **hunt** 動狩る, 狩りをする, 探し求める 名狩り, 追跡
- **hunter** 名①狩りをする人, 狩人, ハンター ②猟馬, 猟犬
- **hunting whip** 狩猟用むち
- **hurry** 熟 in a hurry 急いで, あわてて
- **husband** 熟 make a good husband よい夫になる
- **hut** 名簡易住居, あばら屋, 山小屋

I

- **I give you my word.** 約束するよ。保証するよ。
- **if** 熟 as if あたかも～のように
- **illness** 名病気
- **imagine** 動想像する, 心に思い描く
- **immediate** 形さっそくの, 即座の, 直接の
- **immediately** 副すぐに, ～するやいなや
- **impatient** 形我慢できない, いらいらしている
- **improve** 動改善する［させる］, 進歩する
- **in** 熟 in a hurry 急いで, あわてて in charge of ～を任されて, ～を預かって in control ～を支配して, ～を掌握している in honor of ～を祝って in one hour 1時間で, 1時間以内に in one place 一ヶ所に in order to ～するために in print 紙上に in return お返しとして in the dead of night 真夜中に in time 間に合って pull in (網を)引く show someone in ［人を］中に案内する, 招き入れる
- **include** 動含む, 勘定に入れる

THE HOUND OF THE BASKERVILLES

- [ ] **indeed** 副 ①実際, 本当に ②《強意》まったく 間 本当に, まさか
- [ ] **Indies** 名 West Indies 西インド諸島
- [ ] **inform** 動 ①告げる, 知らせる ② 密告する
- [ ] **initial** 形 最初の, 初めの 名 頭文字 動 頭文字で署名する
- [ ] **insect** 名 虫, 昆虫 insect net 捕虫網
- [ ] **insist** 動 ①主張する, 断言する ② 要求する
- [ ] **instant** 形 即時の, 緊急の, 即席の 名 瞬間, 寸前 in an instant たちまち, ただちに
- [ ] **instantly** 副 すぐに, 即座に
- [ ] **instead** 副 その代わりに instead of ~ ~の代わりに, ~をしないで
- [ ] **intelligent** 形 頭のよい, 聡明な
- [ ] **intend** 動《 – to ~》~しようと思う, ~するつもりである
- [ ] **interested** 形《be》interested in ~に興味[関心]がある
- [ ] **iron** 名 ①鉄, 鉄製のもの ②アイロン 形 鉄の, 鉄製の 動 アイロンをかける
- [ ] **itself** 代 それ自体, それ自身

J

- [ ] **Jack** 名 ジャック《人名》
- [ ] **James** 名 ジェームズ《人名》 James Desmond ジェームズ・デズモンド James Mortimer ジェームズ・モーティマー
- [ ] **John Clayton** ジョン・クレイトン《人名》
- [ ] **joke** 名 冗談, ジョーク 動 冗談を言う, ふざける, からかう
- [ ] **journey** 名 ①(遠い目的地への)旅 ②行程
- [ ] **joy** 喜び, 楽しみ

- [ ] **jump upon** 飛び乗る

K

- [ ] **keep someone from** ~から(人)を阻む
- [ ] **killer** 名 殺人者[犯]
- [ ] **kind** 熟 that is very kind of you ご親切にどうも
- [ ] **kindly** 形 ①親切な, 情け深い, 思いやりのある ②(気候などの)温和な, 快い 副 親切に, 優しく
- [ ] **kiss** 名 キス 動 キスする
- [ ] **kitchen-maid** 名 下働きのメイド
- [ ] **knee** 名 ひざ
- [ ] **Kneller** 名 ゴドフリー・ネラー《肖像画家。Sir Godfrey Kneller》
- [ ] **knock** 動 ノックする, たたく, ぶつける 名 打つこと, 戸をたたくこと[音]
- [ ] **knowingly** 副 すべてお見通しだという顔つきで

L

- [ ] **Lafter Hall** ラフター邸
- [ ] **late** 熟 sooner or later 遅かれ早かれ
- [ ] **lately** 副 近ごろ, 最近
- [ ] **laughter** 名 笑い(声)
- [ ] **Laura Lyons** ローラ・ライオンズ《人名》
- [ ] **lawful** 形 合法な
- [ ] **lay** 動 ①置く, 横たえる, 敷く ②整える ③卵を産む ④lie(横たわる)の過去 lay off レイオフする, 一時解雇する
- [ ] **lead out onto** ~の方へ導く
- [ ] **lean** 動 ①もたれる, 寄りかかる ②

140

傾く, 傾ける lean back 後ろにもたれる 形 やせた, 不毛の
- **leap** 動 ①跳ぶ ②跳び越える 名 跳ぶこと
- **least** 形 いちばん小さい, 最も少ない 副 いちばん小さく, 最も少なく 名 最小, 最少 at least 少なくとも
- **leather** 名 皮革, 皮製品
- **leave behind** 置いて来る
- **led** 動 lead (導く) の過去, 過去分詞
- **length** 名 長さ, 縦, たけ, 距離 at full length 十分に, 全身を伸ばして at length ついに, 詳しく
- **less** 形 ～より小さい[少ない] 副 ～より少なく, ～ほどでなく less and less ～ だんだん少なく～, ますます～でなく no less than ～ ～と同じだけの, ～も同然 not less than ～ ～以下ではなく, ～にまさるとも劣らない 名 より少ない数[量・額]
- **Lestrade** 名 レストレード《人名》
- **lie** 動 ①うそをつく ②横たわる, 寝る ③(ある状態に) ある, 存在する 名 うそ, 詐欺
- **life** 熟 run for one's life 一目散に逃げる
- **lifeless** 形 ①生物の住まない ②生命のない ③活力のない
- **lift** 動 ①持ち上げる, 上がる ②取り除く, 撤廃する 名 ①持ち上げること ②エレベーター, リフト
- **light sleeper** 眠りの浅い人
- **likeable** 形 好ましい
- **lip** 名 唇,《-s》口
- **list** 名 名簿, 目録, 一覧表 動 名簿[目録]に記入する
- **live out** 生き延びる
- **lively** 形 ①元気のよい, 活発な ②鮮やかな, 強烈な, 真に迫った
- **London** 名 ロンドン《英国の首都》
- **lonely** 形 ①孤独な, 心さびしい ②ひっそりした, 人里離れた
- **longer** 熟 no longer もはや でない
- **look** 熟 look around for ～を捜し求める look for ～を探す look in 中を見る, 立ち寄る look into ～ をのぞき込む look out over ～をはるかに見渡す
- **loose** 形 自由な, ゆるんだ, あいまいな 動 ほどく, 解き放つ
- **loss** 名 ①損失(額・物), 損害, 浪費 ②失敗, 敗北 at a loss 途方に暮れて
- **lovely** 形 愛らしい, 美しい, すばらしい
- **lying** 動 lie (うそをつく・横たわる) の現在分詞 形 ①うそをつく, 虚偽の ②横になっている 名 ①うそをつくこと, 虚言, 虚偽 ②横たわること
- **Lyons** 名 Laura Lyons ローラ・ライオンズ《人名》

M

- **M.R.C.S.** 略 Membership of the Royal College of Surgeons 王立外科医学協会準会員
- **madam** 名《ていねいな呼びかけ》奥様, お嬢様
- **madman** 名 ①狂人 ②常軌を逸した人
- **maid** 名 お手伝い, メイド
- **mainly** 副 主に
- **make** 熟《be》made up of ～ で構成されている make a good husband よい夫になる
- **man** 熟 man of science 科学者
- **manager** 名 経営者, 支配人, 支店長, 部長
- **manner** 名 ①方法, やり方 ②態度, 様子 ③《-s》行儀, 作法, 生活様式
- **manor** 名 ①荘園 ②警察の管轄区
- **manuscript** 名 原稿, 手書き原稿, 写本

THE HOUND OF THE BASKERVILLES

- **mark** 名①印, 記号, 跡 ②点数 ③特色 動①印[記号]をつける ②採点する ③目立たせる
- **marker** 名 dry-land marker stick 乾燥地の目印棒
- **marriage** 名①結婚(生活・式) ②結合, 融合, (吸収)合併
- **marry** 動結婚する
- **master** 名主人, 雇い主, 師, 名匠 動①修得する ②〜の主となる
- **match** 名①試合, 勝負 ②相手, 釣り合うもの ③マッチ(棒) 動①(〜を…と)勝負させる ②調和する, 釣り合う match up to 〜 〜と合致[匹敵]する
- **meantime** 名合間, その間 副その間に
- **meanwhile** 副それまでの間, 一方では
- **medical** 形①医学の ②内科の Medical Directory 医師録 Medical Officer 医官 名健康診断, 身体検査
- **memory** 名①記憶(力), 思い出 ②(コンピュータの)メモリ, 記憶装置
- **mental** 形①心の, 精神の ②知能[知性]の
- **mention** 動(〜について)述べる, 言及する Don't mention it. どういたしまして。 名言及, 陳述
- **Merripit House** メリピット荘
- **messenger** 名使者, (伝言・小包などの)配達人, 伝達者 messenger office メッセンジャー会社
- **metal** 名金属, 合金
- **middle** 名中間, 最中 形中間の, 中央の
- **midnight** 名夜の12時, 真夜中, 暗黒 形真夜中の, 真っ暗な
- **might** 動《mayの過去》①〜かもしれない ②〜してもよい, 〜できる 名力, 権力

- **mile** 名①マイル《長さの単位。1,609m》②《-s》かなりの距離
- **mind** 名①心, 精神, 考え ②知性 make up one's mind 決心する 動①気にする, いやがる ②気をつける, 用心する Never mind. 心配するな。
- **mine** 名鉱坑
- **mire** 名沼地 Grimpen Mire グリンペン大沼
- **mistaken** 動 mistake(間違える)の過去分詞 形誤った
- **mix** 動①混ざる, 混ぜる ②(〜を)一緒にする 名混合(物)
- **modern** 形現代[近代]の, 現代的な, 最近の 名現代[近代]人
- **moment** 名①瞬間, ちょっとの間 ②(特定の)時, 時期 at any moment いつ何時, 今にも at the moment 今は in a moment ただちに
- **mood** 名気分, 機嫌, 雰囲気, 憂うつ
- **moonlight** 名月明かり, 月光
- **moor** 名原野, 沼地 動停泊する[させる]
- **Mortimer** 名 James Mortimer ジェームズ・モーティマー《人名》
- **movement** 名①動き, 運動 ②《-s》行動 ③引っ越し ④変動
- **murder** 名人殺し, 殺害, 殺人事件 動殺す
- **murderer** 名殺人犯
- **murderous** 形残忍な
- **murmuring** 形うめく(音)
- **My God.** 間おや, まあ
- **mysterious** 形神秘的な, 謎めいた
- **mystery** 名①神秘, 不可思議 ②推理小説, ミステリー

142

WORD LIST

N

- **narrow** 形 ①狭い ②限られた 動 狭くなる[する]
- **natural scientist** 自然科学者, 博物学者
- **naturalist** 名 ①自然主義者 ②博物学者
- **nearby** 形 近くの, 間近の 近くで, 間近で
- **nearly** 副 ①近くに, 親しく ②ほとんど, あやうく
- **necessary** 形 必要な, 必然の if necessary もし必要ならば 名《-s》必需品, 必需品
- **neither** 形 どちらの〜も…でない 代《2者のうち》どちらも〜でない 副《否定文に続いて》〜も…しない
- **nephew** 名 おい(甥)
- **nerve** 名 ①神経 ②気力, 精力 ③《-s》神経過敏, 臆病, 憂うつ
- **nervous** 形 ①神経の ②神経質な, おどおどした nervous breakdown 神経衰弱, ノイローゼ
- **nervously** 副 神経質に, いらいらして
- **net** 名 insect net 捕虫網
- **Never have I seen ...**《倒置》I never have seen ...
- **newspaper** 名 新聞(紙) newspaper type 新聞書体
- **night** 熟 in the dead of night 真夜中に
- **nightclothes** 名 ねまき
- **nobody** 代 誰も[1人も]〜ない 名 とるに足らない人
- **none** 代 (〜の)何も[誰も・少しも]…ない
- **nor** 接 〜もまたない neither 〜 nor … 〜も…もない
- **normal** 形 普通の, 平均の, 標準的な 名 平常, 標準, 典型
- **Northumberland Hotel** ノーサンバーランド・ホテル
- **nosy** 形 おせっかいな
- **note** 名 ①メモ, 覚え書き ②注釈 ③注意, 注目 ④手形 動 ①書き留める ②注意[注目]する
- **Notting Hill** ノッティング・ヒル
- **now** 熟 as of now 今のところ for now 今のところ, ひとまず

O

- **oak** 名 オーク《ブナ科の樹木の総称》 black oak クロガシ 形 オーク(材)の
- **obey** 動 服従する, (命令などに)従う
- **object** 名 ①物, 事物 ②目的物, 対象 動 反対する, 異議を唱える
- **observe** 動 ①観察[観測]する, 監視[注視]する ②気づく ③守る, 遵守する
- **occasion** 名 ①場合, (特定の)時 ②機会, 好機 ③理由, 根拠 on occasion 時折, 時々
- **occasionally** 副 時折, 時たま
- **occur** 動 (事が)起こる, 生じる, (考えなどが)浮かぶ
- **odd** 形 ①奇妙な ②奇数の ③(一対のうちの)片方の
- **off** 熟 carry off さらって行く far off ずっと遠くに, はるかかなたに set off 出発する
- **offer** 動 申し出る, 申し込む, 提供する 名 提案, 提供
- **office** 名 messenger office メッセンジャー会社
- **officer** 名 役人, 公務員, 警察官 Medical Officer 医官
- **oil** 名 ①油, 石油 ②油絵の具, 油絵 動 油を塗る[引く], 滑らかにする
- **old** 形 かつての
- **on** 熟 on one's feet 立っている状

態で on one's way to ～に行く途中で　on the condition that もし～なら　on which = where
- **one another** お互い
- **onto** 前 ～の上へ[に]
- **opportunity** 名 好機, 適当な時期[状況]
- **order** in order to ～するために
- **ought** 助 《–to～》当然～すべきである, きっと～するはずである
- **out** lead out onto ～の方へ導く live out 生き延びる look out over ～をはるかに見渡す point out ～に目を向けさせる put out (明かり・火を)消す speak out はっきり[遠慮なく]言う stare out ～をじっと見つめる
- **outdoors** 副 戸外で 名《the–》戸外, 野外
- **Oxford Street** オックスフォード街

P

- **package** 名 包み, 小包, パッケージ 動 包装する, 荷造りする
- **Paddington** 名 パディントン駅
- **paid** 動 pay (払う) の過去, 過去分詞 形 有給の, 支払い済みの
- **painful** 形 ①痛い, 苦しい, 痛ましい ②骨の折れる, 困難な
- **pair** 名 (2つから成る)一対, 一組, ペア 動 対になる[する]
- **pale** 形 ①(顔色・人が)青ざめた, 青白い ②(色が)薄い, (光が)薄暗い 動 ①青ざめる, 青ざめさせる ②淡くなる[する], 色あせる
- **paper** 名 unsigned police papers 署名なしの逮捕状
- **particular** 形 ①特別の ②詳細な 名 事項, 細部,《-s》詳細 in particular 特に, とりわけ
- **pass for** ～で通る
- **passenger** 名 乗客, 旅客
- **passion** 名 情熱, (～への)熱中, 激怒
- **passionately** 副 激しく, 吐き出すように
- **past** 形 過去の, この前の 名 過去(の出来事) 前《時間・場所》～を過ぎて, ～を越して 副 通り越して, 過ぎて
- **path** 名 ①(踏まれてできた)小道, 歩道 ②進路, 通路
- **patience** 名 我慢, 忍耐(力), 根気
- **patient** 形 我慢[忍耐]強い, 根気のある 名 病人, 患者
- **pay** 動 ①支払う, 払う, 償う ②割に合う, ペイする 名 給料, 報い
- **perfectly** 副 完全に, 申し分なく
- **perfume** 名 香り, 香水 動 香水をつける
- **perhaps** 副 たぶん, ことによると
- **Perkins** 名 パーキンス《人名》
- **personal** 形 ①個人の ②本人自らの ③容姿の
- **phosphorous** 名 リン
- **photograph** 名 写真 動 写真を撮る
- **physical** 形 ①物質の, 物理学の, 自然科学の ②身体の, 肉体の
- **physically** 副 ①自然法則上, 物理的に ②肉体的に, 身体的に
- **pile** 名 積み重ね, (～の)山 動 積み重ねる, 積もる
- **pity** 名 哀れみ, 同情, 残念なこと 動 気の毒に思う, 哀れむ
- **place** 熟 in one place 一ヶ所に take one's place (人の)代わりをする
- **pleasant** 形 ①(物事が)楽しい, 心地よい ②快活な, 愛想のよい
- **pleasure** 名 喜び, 楽しみ, 満足, 娯楽 (It's) my pleasure. どういた

WORD LIST

しまして。

- **pocketbook** 名 ①札入れ, ハンドバッグ ②手帳 ③文庫本
- **point** 熟 point out 〜に目を向けさせる There's no point in 〜しても意味がない
- **pole** 名 ①棒, さお, 柱 ②極(地), 電極
- **police** unsigned police papers 署名なしの逮捕状
- **portrait** 名 肖像画
- **position** 名 ①位置, 場所, 姿勢 ②地位, 身分, 職 ③立場, 状況 動 置く, 配置する
- **positive** 形 ①積極的な ②明確な, 明白な, 確信している ③プラスの
- **possession** 名 所有(物), 財産
- **possible** 形 ①可能な ②ありうる, 起こりうる as 〜 as possible できるだけ〜 if possible できるなら
- **possibly** 副 ①あるいは, たぶん ②《否定文, 疑問文で》どうしても, できる限り, とても, なんとか
- **post-marked** 形 消印済みの
- **postmaster** 名 郵便局長
- **pound** 名 ①ポンド《英国の通貨単位。記号£》②ポンド《重量の単位。453.6g》動 どんどんたたく, 打ち砕く
- **powerful** 形 力強い, 実力のある, 影響力のある
- **practice** 名 (医者の)開業[場所], 診療所
- **prefer** 動 (〜のほうを)好む, (〜のほうが)よいと思う
- **pride** 名 誇り, 自慢, 自尊心 動《–oneself》誇る, 自慢する
- **Princetown Prison** プリンスタウン刑務所
- **print** 熟 in print 紙上に
- **printed word** 活字
- **prison** 名 ①刑務所, 監獄 ②監禁

- **prisoner** 名 囚人, 捕虜
- **private** 形 ①私的な, 個人の ②民間の, 私立の ③内密の, 人里離れた
- **privately** 副 内密に, 非公式に, 個人的に
- **probably** 副 たぶん, あるいは
- **property** 名 ①財産, 所有物[地] ②性質, 属性
- **proud** 形 ①自慢の, 誇った, 自尊心のある ②高慢な, 尊大な
- **prove** 動 ①証明する ②(〜であることが)わかる, (〜と)なる
- **psst** 間 ちょっと, おい
- **publicly** 副 公に, 公然と, 人前で, 世間に
- **pull in** (網を)引く
- **put** 熟 put down 下に置く, ドロす put out (明かり・火を)消す put up one's hand 手を挙げる
- **puzzle** 名 ①難問, 当惑 ②パズル 動 迷わせる, 当惑する[させる]

Q

- **quarter** 名 ①4分の1, 25セント, 15分, 3カ月 ②方面, 地域 ③部署 動 4等分する
- **queer** 形 奇妙な, あやしい, 気分が悪い
- **quickly** 副 敏速に, 急いで
- **quietly** 副 ①静かに ②平穏に, 控えめに

R

- **raincoat** 名 レインコート
- **raise** 動 ①上げる, 高める ②起こす ③〜を育てる ④(資金を)調達する 名 高める[上げる]こと, 昇給
- **rang** 動 ring (鳴る)の過去

THE HOUND OF THE BASKERVILLES

- **rather** 副 ①むしろ, かえって ②かなり, いくぶん, やや ③それどころか逆に would rather ～ than …… …よりむしろ～したい
- **reach for** ～に手を伸ばす, ～を取ろうとする
- **realize** 動 理解する, 実現する
- **reasonable** 形 筋の通った, 分別のある
- **rebuilt** 動 rebuild (再建する) の過去, 過去分詞
- **recent** 形 近ごろの, 近代の
- **recently** 副 近ごろ, 最近
- **recognize** 動 認める, 認識[承認]する
- **record** 名 ①記録, 登録, 履歴 ②(音楽などの) レコード off the record 非公式で, オフレコで on record 記録されて, 公表されて 動 ①記録[登録]する ②録音[録画]する
- **recover** 動 ①取り戻す, ばん回する ②回復する
- **reddish** 形 赤みがかった
- **red-faced** 形 赤ら顔の
- **redness** 名 赤み
- **refuse** 動 拒絶する, 断る 名 くず, 廃物
- **regard** 動 ①(～を…と) 見なす ②尊敬する, 重きを置く ③関係がある 名 ①注意, 関心, 尊敬, 好感 ③《-s》(手紙などで) よろしくというあいさつ in [with] regard to ～ ～に関しては without regard to [for] ～ ～を無視して
- **Regent Street** リージェント街
- **region** 名 ①地方, 地域 ②範囲
- **registered post** 書留郵便
- **rejoin** 動 復帰する, 再び一緒になる
- **relation** 名 ①(利害) 関係, 間柄 ②親戚
- **relief** 名 (苦痛・心配などの) 除去, 軽減, 安心, 気晴らし
- **remain** 動 ①残っている, 残る ②(～の) ままである[いる] 名《-s》①残り (もの) ②遺跡
- **remark** 名 ①注意, 注目, 観察 ②意見, 記事, 批評 動 ①注目する ②述べる, 批評する
- **remove** 動 ①取り去る, 除去する ②(衣類を) 脱ぐ
- **repeat** 繰り返す 名 繰り返し, 反復, 再演
- **respect** 名 ①尊敬, 尊重 ②注意, 考慮 動 尊敬[尊重]する
- **restore** 動 元に戻す, 復活させる
- **result** 名 結果, 成り行き, 成績 as a result その結果(として) as a result of ～ ～の結果(として) 動 (結果として)起こる, 生じる, 結局～になる
- **return** 熟 in return お返しとして
- **Reynolds** 名 ジョシュア・レイノルズ《肖像画家。Sir Joshua Reynolds》
- **rider** 名 (自転車・オートバイ・馬などの) 乗り手, ライダー
- **rifle** 名 ライフル銃
- **ring** 名 ①輪, 円形, 指輪 ②競技場, リング 動 ①輪で取り囲む ②鳴る, 鳴らす ③電話をかける
- **roar** 動 ①ほえる ②(人が) わめく ③鳴り響く 名 ①ほえ声, 怒号 ②大笑い
- **rocky** 形 ①岩の多い ②ぐらぐら揺れる, ぐらつく
- **rode** ride (乗る) の過去
- **Rodger Baskerville** ロジャー・バスカヴィル《人名》
- **roll** 動 ①転がる, 転がす ②(波などが) うねる, 横揺れする ③(時が) たつ 名 ①一巻き ②名簿, 目録
- **roof** 名 屋根 (のようなもの), 住居 動 屋根をつける
- **room** 名 dining room 食堂
- **rough** 形 ①(手触りが) 粗い ②

荒々しい, 未加工の
- **rough-looking** 形 見かけの粗野な
- **route** 名 道, 道筋, 進路, 回路
- **rub** 動 ①こする, こすって磨く ②すりむく 名 摩擦
- **ruin** 名 破滅, 滅亡, 破産, 廃墟 動 破滅させる
- **run** 熟 run away 走り去る, 逃げ出す run for one's life 一目散に逃げる

S

- **saddened** 形 悲しみに包まれた
- **sadly** 副 悲しそうに, 不幸にも
- **sadness** 名 悲しみ, 悲哀
- **safely** 副 安全に, 間違いなく
- **safety** 名 安全, 無事, 確実
- **sank** 動 sink (沈む) の過去
- **satisfy** 動 ①満足させる, 納得させる ②(義務を) 果たす, 償う
- **scare** 動 こわがらせる, おびえる 名 恐れ, 不安
- **scenery** 名 風景, 景色
- **schoolmaster** 名 ①先生 ②校長
- **science** 名 man of science 科学者
- **scientist** 名 natural scientist 自然科学者, 博物学者
- **scream** 名 金切り声, 絶叫 動 叫ぶ, 金切り声を出す
- **search** 動 捜し求める, 調べる 名 捜査, 探索, 調査
- **secret** 形 ①秘密の, 隠れた ②神秘の, 不思議な 名 秘密, 神秘
- **secretly** 副 秘密に, 内緒で
- **seem** 動 (〜に) 見える, (〜のように) 思われる
- **Selden** 名 セルデン《名》

- **send for** 〜を呼びにやる, 〜を呼び寄せる
- **sense** 名 ①感覚, 感じ ②《-s》意識, 正気, 本性 ③常識, 分別, センス ④意味 in a sense ある意味では make sense 意味をなす, よくわかる 動 感じる, 気づく
- **sentence** 名 ①文 ②判決, 宣告 動 判決を下す, 宣告する
- **separate** 動 ①分ける, 分かれる, 隔てる ②別れる, 別れさせる 形 分かれた, 別れた, 別々の
- **separation** 名 分離 (点), 離脱, 分類, 別離
- **serious** 形 ①まじめな, 真剣な ②重大な, 深刻な, (病気などが) 重い
- **serious-looking** 形 しかつめらしい
- **servant** 名 ①召使, 使用人, しもべ ②公務員, (公共事業の) 従業員
- **serve** 動 ①仕える, 奉仕する ②(客の) 応対をする, 給仕する, 食事 [飲み物] を出す ③(役目を) 果たす, 務める, 役に立つ ④(球技で) サーブをする 名 (球技で) サーブ (権)
- **service** 名 ①勤務, 業務 ②公益事業 ③点検, 修理 ④奉仕, 貢献 《**be** of service to》〜の手助けになる 動 保守点検する, (点検) 修理をする
- **set** 熟 set off 出発する
- **shadow** 名 ①影, 暗がり ②亡霊 動 ①陰にする, 暗くする ②尾行する
- **shadowy** 形 影のある, 陰の多い, 暗い, おぼろげな
- **shake** 熟 《**be**》shaken to the soul 心の底から震える
- **shaken** 動 shake (振る) の過去分詞
- **shamefully** 副 恥ずかしくも, 不面目に
- **shape** 名 ①形, 姿, 型 ②状態, 調子 動 形づくる, 具体化する shape up 具体化する, 調子がよくなる
- **sharp** 形 ①鋭い, とがった ②刺す

- ような, きつい ③鋭敏な ④急な 副 ①鋭く, 急に ②(時間が)ちょうど
- **sharply** 副 鋭く, 激しく, はっきりと
- **sheep** 名 羊
- **sheet** 名 ①シーツ ②(紙などの)1枚
- **Sherlock Holmes** シャーロック・ホームズ《人名》
- **shilling** 名 シリング《英国の旧通貨単位。1/20ポンド》
- **shine** 動 ①光る, 輝く ②光らせる, 磨く 名 光, 輝き
- **shook** 動 shake(振る)の過去
- **shortly** 副 まもなく, すぐに
- **shoulder** 名 肩 動 肩にかつぐ, 肩で押し分けて進む
- **show someone in** [人を]中に案内する, 招き入れる
- **shy** 形 内気な, 恥ずかしがりの, 臆病な
- **side** 名 側, 横, そば, 斜面 side by side 並んで 形 ①側面の, 横の ②副次的な 動 (〜の)側につく, 賛成する
- **sigh** 動 ①ため息をつく, ため息をついて言う ②(風が)そよぐ 名 ①ため息 ②(風の)そよぐ音
- **signal** 名 信号, 合図, 信号機 動 信号を送る, 合図する
- **silence** 名 沈黙, 無言, 静寂 in silence 黙って, 沈黙のうちに 動 沈黙させる, 静める
- **silent** 形 ①無言の, 黙っている ②静かな, 音を立てない ③活動しない
- **silently** 副 静かに, 黙って
- **silk** 名 絹(布), 生糸 形 絹の, 絹製の
- **silver** 名 銀, 銀貨, 銀色 形 銀製の
- **similar** 形 同じような, 類似した, 相似の
- **simply** 副 ①簡単に ②単に, ただ ③まったく, 完全に
- **since** 熟 ever since その後ずっと
- **single** 形 ①たった1つの ②1人用の, それぞれの ③独身の ④片道の 名 ①片道乗車券 ②(ホテルなどの)1人用の部屋 ③《-s》(テニスなどの)シングルス
- **sit up** 起き上がる, 上半身を起こす
- **sitting room** 居間
- **situation** 名 ①場所, 位置 ②状況, 境遇, 立場
- **sleeper** 名 眠っている人[動物, 植物] light sleeper 眠りの浅い人
- **slightly** 副 わずかに, いささか
- **slowly** 副 遅く, ゆっくり
- **smoke** 動 喫煙する, 煙を出す smoke out いぶり出す, 明るみに出す 名 煙, 煙状のもの
- **smoking room** 喫煙室
- **smooth** 形 滑らかな, すべすべした 動 滑らかにする, 平らにする
- **so** 熟 so that 〜できるように so 〜 that … 非常に〜なので…
- **soften** 動 柔らかくなる[する], 和らぐ
- **softly** 副 柔らかに, 優しく, そっと
- **soldier** 名 兵士, 兵卒
- **somebody** 代 誰か, ある人 名 ひとかどの人物, 大物
- **somehow** 副 ①どうにかこうにか, ともかく, 何とかして ②どういうわけか
- **someone** 代 ある人, 誰か
- **something** 代 ①ある物, 何か ②いくぶん, 多少
- **sometimes** 副 時々, 時たま
- **somewhat** 副 いくらか, やや, 多少
- **somewhere** 副 ①どこかへ[に] ②いつか, およそ
- **sooner or later** 遅かれ早かれ
- **sorrow** 名 悲しみ, 後悔

WORD LIST

- **soul** 名 ①魂 ②精神, 心 《be》 shaken to the soul 心の底から震える
- **spaniel** 名 スパニエル犬
- **speak** 熟 speak out はっきり[遠慮なく]言う speak up 率直に話す, はっきりしゃべる
- **speed** 名 速力, 速度 動 ①急ぐ, 急がせる ②制限速度以上で走る, スピード違反をする
- **spirit** 名 ①霊 ②精神, 気力
- **spoil** 動 ①台なしにする, だめになる, だめになる ②甘やかす
- **spot** 名 ①地点, 場所, 立場 ②斑点, しみ on the spot その場で, ただちに 動 ①〜を見つける ②点を打つ, しみをつける
- **spy** 名 スパイ 動 ひそかに見張る, スパイする
- **square** 名 ①正方形, 四角い広場, (市外の) 一区画 ②2乗, 平方 形 ①正方形の, 四角な, 直角な, 角ばった ②平方の 動 ①四角[直角]にする ②2乗する
- **sshh** 間 しーっ
- **St. Oliver's Private scool** セント・オリバー私立学校
- **stair** 名 ①(階段の)1段 ②《-s》階段, はしご
- **Stapleton** 名 ステイプルトン《人名》
- **stare** 動 じっと[じろじろ]見る stare out 〜をじっと見つめる 名 じっと見ること, 凝視
- **steep** 形 険しい, 法外な 動 漬ける, 浸っている
- **stick** 名 棒, 杖 dry-land marker stick 乾燥地の目印棒 guiding stick 目印の棒 walking stick 杖, ステッキ 動 ①(突き)刺さる, 刺す ②くっつく, くっつける ③突き出る ④《受け身形で》いきづまる
- **stole** 動 steal (盗む) の過去
- **stone** 名 ①石, 小石 ②宝石 stone circles 環状列石 形 石の, 石製の
- **storekeeper** 名 店主, 店長, 小売り商人
- **stormy** 形 ①嵐の, 暴風の ②激しい
- **strangely** 副 奇妙に, 変に, 不思議なことに, 不慣れに
- **stranger** 名 ①見知らぬ人, 他人 ②不案内[不慣れ]な人
- **street** 名 Oxford Street オックスフォード街 Regent Street リージェント街
- **strength** 名 ①力, 体力 ②長所, 強み ③強度, 濃度
- **strike** 動 ①打つ, ぶつかる ②(災害などが)急に襲う strike back 打ち返す, 仕返しする strike off 削除する, 除名する strike on 〜を思いつく 名 ①ストライキ ②打つこと, 打撃
- **strip** 動 裸にする, 脱衣する, はぐ, 取り去る 名 《細長い》1片
- **strong-looking** 形 強そうに見える, 頑健そうな
- **struck** 動 strike (打つ) の過去, 過去分詞
- **study** 名 書斎
- **stupid** 形 ばかな, おもしろくない
- **substance** 名 ①物質, 物 ②実質, 中身, 内容
- **succeed** 動 ①成功する ②(〜の)跡を継ぐ
- **success** 名 成功, 幸運, 上首尾
- **successful** 形 成功した, うまくいった
- **sudden** 形 突然の, 急な
- **suffer** 動 ①(苦痛・損害などを)受ける, こうむる ②(病気に)なる, 苦しむ, 悩む
- **suggest** 動 ①暗示する ②提案する
- **suit** 名 ①スーツ, 背広 ②訴訟 ③ひとそろい, 一組 動 ①適合する[さ

せる] ②似合う
- □ **supernatural** 形 超自然の
- □ **supply** 動 供給[配給]する, 補充する 名 供給(品), 給与, 補充
- □ **support** 動 ①支える, 支持する ②養う, 援助する 名 ①支え, 支持 ②援助, 扶養
- □ **suppose** 動 ①仮定する, 推測する ②《be -d to ~》~することになっている, ~するものである
- □ **surely** 副 確かに, きっと
- □ **surprisingly** 副 驚くほど(に), 意外にも
- □ **surround** 動 囲む, 包囲する
- □ **suspect** 動 疑う, (~ではないかと)思う 名 容疑者, 注意人物
- □ **swept** 動 sweep (掃く)の過去, 過去分詞

T

- □ **take** 熟 take a chance 一か八かやってみる take one's place (人の)代わりをする
- □ **tale** 名 ①話, 物語 ②うわさ, 悪口
- □ **taste** 名 ①味, 風味 ②好み, 趣味 動 味がする, 味わう
- □ **tax** 名 ①税 ②重荷, 重い負担 動 ①課税する ②重荷を負わせる
- □ **teenager** 名 10代の人, ティーンエイジャー《13歳から19歳》
- □ **telegram** 名 電報 動 電報を打つ
- □ **telegraph** 名 電報, 電信 動 電報を打つ
- □ **telescope** 名 望遠鏡
- □ **tell of** ~について話す[説明する]
- □ **temper** 名 ①気質, 気性, 気分 ②短気 keep one's temper 平静さを保つ lose one's temper かんしゃくを起こす
- □ **temple** 名 ①寺, 神殿 ②こめかみ
- □ **terribly** 副 ひどく
- □ **Thank God.** ありがたい
- □ **that** 熟 so that ~できるように so ~ that … 非常に~なので…
- □ **theory** 名 理論, 学説
- □ **there** 熟 there goes [チャンスなどが] 行ってしまう There's no point in ~ しても意味がない
- □ **therefore** 副 したがって, それゆえ, その結果
- □ **thick** 形 厚い, 密集した, 濃厚な 副 厚く, 濃く 名 最も厚い[強い・濃い]部分
- □ **thin** 形 薄い, 細い, やせた, まばらな 副 薄く 動 薄く[細く]なる, 薄くする
- □ **think of** ~を思いつく
- □ **Thorsley** 名 トースリー《地名》
- □ **though** 接 ①~にもかかわらず, ~だが ②たとえ~でも 副 しかし
- □ **thread** 名 糸, 糸のように細いもの 動 糸を通す
- □ **throat** 名 のど, 気管
- □ **throw down** 投げ出す, 放棄する
- □ **tightly** 副 きつく, しっかり, 堅く
- □ **time** 熟 in time 間に合って
- □ **tiny** 形 ちっぽけな, とても小さい
- □ **tip** 名 ①チップ, 心づけ ②先端, 頂点 動 ①チップをやる ②先端につける
- □ **title** 名 ①題名, タイトル ②肩書, 称号 ②権利, 資格 動 題をつける, 肩書を与える
- □ **tobacco** 名 たばこ
- □ **tone** 名 音, 音色, 調子 動 調和する[させる]
- □ **tor** 名 ゴツゴツした岩山
- □ **total** 形 総計の, 全体の, 完全な 名 全体, 合計 動 合計する
- □ **tragedy** 名 悲劇, 惨劇
- □ **treat** 動 ①扱う ②治療する ③お

Word List

- ごる 名 ①おごり, もてなし, ごちそう ②楽しみ
- **tree-lined** 形 並木のある
- **trick** 名 ①策略 ②いたずら, 冗談 ③手品, 錯覚 動 だます
- **trouble** 熟 get into trouble with ~とトラブルを起こす
- **truly** 副 本当に, 心から
- **trust** 動 信用[信頼]する, 委託する 名 信用, 信頼, 委託
- **trusty** 形 信頼できる
- **truth** 名 ①真理, 事実, 本当 ②誠実, 忠実さ to tell the truth 実は, 実を言えば
- **turn in** 床につく
- **twin** 名 双子の一方, 双生児, よく似た1対の人の一方 形 双子の, 1対の
- **type** 名 newspaper type 新聞書体
- **typewriter** 名 タイプライター

U

- **ugly** 形 ①醜い, ぶかっこうな ②いやな, 不快な, 険悪な
- **um** 間 ううん, ううむ
- **unable** 形《be – to ~》~することができない
- **unbelievable** 形 信じられない (ほどの), 度のはずれた
- **unbelievably** 副 信じられないほど
- **uncertain** 形 不確かな, 確信がない
- **uncomfortably** 副 心地悪く
- **uncommon** 形 珍しい, まれな
- **unconcerned** 形 無関心な, 心配しない
- **uncover** 動 ふたを取る, 覆いを取る
- **uneasy** 形 不安な, 焦って
- **unemotional** 形 感情的でない
- **unexpected** 形 思いがけない, 予期しない
- **unfair** 形 不公平な, 不当な
- **unfold** 動 ①(折りたたんだものを)広げる, 開く ②(計画などを)知らせる, 明らかになる
- **ungodly** 副 邪悪な
- **unhappy** 形 不運な, 不幸な
- **unknown** 形 知られていない, 不明の
- **unless** 接 もし~でなければ, ~しなければ
- **unlikely** 形 ありそうもない, 考えられない
- **unlock** 動 かぎを開ける, 解く
- **unmarried** 形 未婚の, 独身の
- **unpleasant** 形 不愉快な, 気にさわる, いやな, 不快
- **unprotected** 形 ①無防備な ②保護のない
- **unsigned police papers** 署名なしの逮捕状
- **unusual** 形 普通でない, 珍しい, 見[聞き]慣れない
- **up** 熟《be》made up of ~で構成されている sit up 起き上がる, 上半身を起こす speak up 率直に話す, はっきりしゃべる
- **upon** 前 ①《場所・接触》~(の上)に ②《日・時》~に ③《関係・従事》~に関して, ~について, ~して 副 前へ, 続けて
- **upper floor** 上階
- **upset** 形 憤慨して, 動揺して 動 気を悪くさせる, (心・神経など)をかき乱す
- **upstairs** 副 2階へ[に], 階上に 形 2階の, 階上の 名 2階, 階上
- **used** 熟 get used to ~に慣れる
- **usual** 形 通常の, いつもの, 平常の, 普通の as usual いつものように, 相変わらず

THE HOUND OF THE BASKERVILLES

V

- **valley** 名 谷, 谷間
- **value** 名 価値, 値打ち, 価格 of value 貴重な, 価値のある 動 評価する, 値をつける, 大切にする
- **Vandeleur** 名 ヴァンデリュル《人名》
- **victory** 名 勝利, 優勝
- **villain** 名 悪党, 悪者, 罪人
- **visitor** 名 訪問客
- **voyage** 名 航海, 航行, 空の旅 動 航海する, 空の旅をする

W

- **wagon** 名 荷馬車, ワゴン(車)
- **wait for** 〜を待つ
- **walk upon** 〜の上を歩く
- **walking stick** 杖, ステッキ
- **warn** 動 警告する, 用心させる warn of 〜を警告する
- **waste-basket** 名 くずかご
- **wastepaper** 名 紙くず
- **watchmen** 名 watchman (夜警) の複数
- **Waterloo** 名 ウォータールー駅
- **Watson** 名 ワトソン《人名》
- **way** 熟 on one's way to 〜に行く途中で
- **wealth** 名 ①富, 財産 ②豊富, 多量
- **well-being** 名 快適な暮らし, 幸福, 福祉
- **well-educated** 形 教養のある
- **well-known** 形 よく知られた, 有名な
- **well-trained** 形 よく訓練された
- **West Indies** 西インド諸島
- **Westmoreland** 名 ウエストモアランド《地名》
- **wet** 形 ぬれた, 湿った, 雨の 動 ぬらす, ぬれる
- **whatever** 代 ①《関係代名詞》〜するものは何でも ②どんなこと[もの]が〜とも 形 ①どんな〜でも ②《否定文・疑問文で》少しの〜も, 何らかの
- **whether** 接 〜かどうか, 〜かまたは…, 〜であろうとなかろうと whether or not 〜かどうか
- **which** 熟 on which = where
- **whip** 動 ①むちうつ ②急に動く[動かす] 名 むち
- **whiskey** 名 ウイスキー
- **whisper** 動 ささやく, 小声で話す 名 ささやき, ひそひそ話, うわさ
- **white with anger** 怒りで顔色が白くなる
- **white-haired** 形 白髪の
- **whoa** 間 おっと, うわっ
- **whole** 形 全体の, すべての, 完全な, 満の, 丸ー 名 《the -》全体, 全部 as a whole 全体として on the whole 全体として見ると
- **whom** 代 ①誰を[に] ②《関係代名詞》〜するところの人, そしてその人を By whom? 誰に?
- **wide** 形 幅の広い, 大範囲の, 幅が〜ある 副 広く, 大きく開いて
- **wildly** 副 荒々しく, 乱暴に, むやみに
- **will** 遺言(状)
- **William Baskerville** ウィリアム・バスカヴィル《人名》
- **wine** 名 ワイン, ぶどう酒
- **wing** 名 翼, 羽
- **wire** 名 ①針金, 電線 ②電信 動 電報を打つ, 配線をする
- **wish** 熟 I wish I had been there. 自分がそこにいられればよかったのに。

- ☐ **witness** 名 ①証拠, 証言 ②目撃者 動 ①目撃する ②証言する
- ☐ **woke** 動 wake（目が覚める）の過去
- ☐ **wonder** 動 ①不思議に思う,（〜に）驚く ②（〜かしらと）思う 名 驚き（の念）, 不思議なもの
- ☐ **wooden** 形 木製の, 木でできた
- ☐ **wool** 名 羊毛, 毛糸, 織物, ウール
- ☐ **word** 名 I give you my word. 約束するよ。保証するよ。 printed word 活字
- ☐ **worker** 名 働く人, 労働者
- ☐ **worse** 形 いっそう悪い, より劣った, よりひどい 副 いっそう悪く
- ☐ **worst** 形《the –》最も悪い, いちばんひどい 副 最も悪く, いちばんひどく 名《the –》最悪の事態［人・物］
- ☐ **writer** 名 書き手, 作家

Y

- ☐ **yard** 名 ヤード《長さの単位。0.9144m》
- ☐ **yew tree** イチイ
- ☐ **york** 名 ヨーク《地名》
- ☐ **yorkshire** 名 ヨークシャー《地名》
- ☐ **younger brother** 弟

E-CAT

English Conversational Ability Test
国際英語会話能力検定

● E-CATとは…

英語が話せるようになるための
テストです。インターネット
ベースで、30分であなたの発
話力をチェックします。

www.ecatexam.com

iTEP

● iTEP®とは…

世界各国の企業、政府機関、アメリカの大学
300校以上が、英語能力判定テストとして採用。
オンラインによる90分のテストで文法、リー
ディング、リスニング、ライティング、スピー
キングの5技能をスコア化。iTEP®は、留学、就
職、海外赴任などに必要な、世界に通用する英
語力を総合的に評価する画期的なテストです。

www.itepexamjapan.com

ラダーシリーズ
The Hound of the Baskervilles
シャーロック・ホームズ／バスカヴィル家の犬

2010年 2月7日　第1刷発行
2020年10月8日　第3刷発行

原著者　コナン・ドイル

発行者　浦　晋亮

発行所　IBCパブリッシング株式会社
　　　　〒162-0804 東京都新宿区中里町29番3号
　　　　菱秀神楽坂ビル9F
　　　　Tel. 03-3513-4511　Fax. 03-3513-4512
　　　　www.ibcpub.co.jp

© IBC Publishing, Inc. 2009

印刷　株式会社シナノパブリッシングプレス
装丁　伊藤 理恵　　カバーイラスト　田口 智子
組版データ　Berkeley Oldstyle Medium+Berkeley Oldstyle Italic

落丁本・乱丁本は、小社宛にお送りください。送料小社負担にてお取り替えいたします。
本書の無断複写（コピー）は著作権法上での例外を除き禁じられています。

Printed in Japan
ISBN 978-4-7946-0030-1